The power of
ULTRASONICS

Fridus van der Weijden

quintessence
books

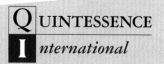
QUINTESSENCE
International

This book is dedicated to Gordon Wolffe, my teacher, colleague, and friend.

Author:

Fridus van der Weijden

First published in 2005 by Academisch Centrum Tandheelkunde Amsterdam (ACTA) in Dutch: *De stille kracht van ultrasoon*.

ISBN number: 978-2-912550-51-4

Appreciation goes to the many contributors.

A special note of gratitude goes to:

Dick Barendregt
Wil Heeffer
Martijn Rosema
Luc van der Sluis
Gordon Wolffe

Photography:

Klaas Jan van Egmond, *ACTA*

Design:

Beebs van Riessen, *ACTA*

© 2007 Quintessence International

Quintessence International
11 bis, rue d'Aguesseau
75008 Paris
France

CONTENTS

INTRODUCTION

Periodontal therapy aims at healing the infected and inflamed gingival tissue as well as preventing further progression of the infection within the periodontium. This objective can be achieved by meticulous professional debridement, which requires the removal of supra- and subgingival plaque and calculus. This will result in the gingiva becoming tightly adapted to the cervical margins of the teeth. For the operator, success is clinically visible as pocket-depth reduction and a reduction of the bleeding on probing. Periodic mechanical removal of supra- and subgingival bacterial plaque is essential for keeping the periodontal infection under control. Following initial therapy and after a number of weeks, periodontopathic microorganisms may be able to recolonize the pocket. In advanced periodontal problems, where the subgingival root surface area must be cleaned carefully and thoroughly to remove all bacterial deposits, this professional debridement is quite difficult. It is a labor-intensive and time-consuming intervention that requires training in order to be carried out adequately. Originally, hand instruments were used for this purpose. During the second half of the last century, electric and air-operated instruments were introduced, which proved to be of great value to the operator for obtaining optimal treatment results. These mechanical scalers are now available in sonic and ultrasonic versions. The vibrations of the (ultra)sonic tip that are transmitted to the tooth surface are responsible for the cleaning effect. The term *ultrasonic* describes a range of acoustic vibrations with a frequency above 20,000 vibrations per second. Humans can detect sounds with frequencies of 20 to 20,000 Hz. Above this limit one speaks of "ultra" sounds: sound that is no longer audible to the human ear. Animals such as bats, dogs, and dolphins, however, are able to hear sounds with frequencies that are higher than 20,000 Hz.

In daily life, an enormous number of sound frequencies are used that are imperceptible to the human ear. These frequencies are used, for example, for car alarms, burglar alarms, and remote controls. In medical applications, high-frequency sound is used in echography for scanning the human body, for instance, during pregnancy. In addition, echography provides more information about the disorders of the salivary glands, such as the presence of cysts and salivary calculi. The physiotherapist makes use of ultrasound against disorders such as inflamed joints and strained muscles. In the dental practice, ultrasonic baths are used for instrument cleaning. Last but not least, ultrasonic instruments are used for professional debridement, the cleaning of root canals, and setting of glass-ionomer cements and in some cases for the preparation of cavities in teeth and bone.

In dentistry, ultrasonic instruments have been in use since the 1950s (Fig 1). In 1952, Balamuth acquired an important patent for the further development and possible uses of ultrasonics. Catuna (1953) suggested that a vibrating ultrasonic tip could be a good replacement for the cord-driven slow handpiece. This ultrasonic instrument worked with a frequency of 29,000 Hz. The tip was placed perpendicular to the tooth surface, and, with the use of an abrasive slurry, enamel and dentine were prepared. According to Postle (1958), ultrasonic preparation was pulp-friendly.

History

Fig 1 Ultrasonic vibrations are sound waves with a frequency ranging from 20,000 Hz to many millions of hertz. Their discovery follows general discoveries in acoustics. Below is a brief overview:

6th century BC
Pythagoras starts with the study of acoustics. His experiments into the properties of vibrating strings were so popular that they led to a "tuning" system that still carries his name: the sonometer of Pythagoras.

4th century BC
Aristotle assumes that a sound wave resonates through the air as a result of vibrations of the air—a hypothesis based rather on philosophical reasoning than on experiments.

1st century BC
Vitruvius determines the correct movement mechanism of sound waves and as an architect makes a large contribution to the acoustic design of theaters.

6th century
The Roman philosopher and politician Boethius describes some ideas in which he connects music to science. He suggests that the perception of tone height is related to the physical properties of the frequency of vibrations.

1883
Galton describes a small whistle which, when blown, produces a high-frequency inaudible sound (up to 100 kHz). This is used by shepherds to direct their sheep dogs.

1915
The French physicist Langevin together with the Russian Chilowsky developed the hydrophone. This is an appliance that is able to detect acoustic energy under water and convert it into electric energy. The appliance is attached to the stern of a ship and produces ultrasonic

vibration waves, which can be sent through water. Fixed objects in the area can be localized by echo reflection of the ultrasonic wave, which ricochets back to the appliance. This device also forms the basis for the medical application of echography.

1926
Boyle and Lehman discover the phenomenon of bubbles in a liquid during the use of an ultrasonic instrument, which was later termed the *cavitation effect*.

However, following the development of the turbine (air-rotor) handpiece, the ultrasonic handpiece totally lost favor in the dental profession (Street, 1959), for a number of reasons:

- Abrasive paste obstructed a clear view of the work field;
- Time needed for preparation was much longer than with the use of the air-rotor;
- Tips were sensitive to wear (rounded tips appeared to be less effective);
- Use of an ultrasonic instrument in combination with the abrasive paste was expensive.

16th and 17th century
Galilee, according to many, is the initiator of modern acoustic research. He took the study of vibrations and the correlation between tone height and the frequency of the source of sound to a scientific level. Elaborating on the basis Galilee had provided, the Frenchman Mersenne studied the vibrations of a tightened string. His results have been summarized in the three laws of Mersenne (Harmonicorum Libri, 1636) and form the basis of modern acoustics.

1822
The Swiss physicist and engineer Colladon and mathematician Sturm tried to calculate the speed of sound in Lake Geneva by means of a bell immersed in water.

1842
Joule discovered the *magnetostrictive effect*. He discovered that certain ferro-magnetic materials, such as iron and nickel, have the ability to change length in a magnetic field.

1880
The Curie brothers generated electricity by placing quartz crystals under pressure. The capacity to convert mechanical energy into electric energy is called the *piëzo-electric effect*.

±1950
At the beginning of the 1950s, ultrasonic instrumentation is introduced by the industry into the field of dentistry as an alternative to the cord-driven, slow handpiece.

1955
Zinner introduces ultrasonic instruments as an aid in periodontal therapy.

1958
The manufacturer Cavitron introduces the "prophylaxis unit," and the brand name develops into a concept. Other applications of ultrasound in dentistry are cleaning of root canals, cleaning of instruments before sterilization, and many more.

The 21st century
Currently, ultrasonic instruments are frequently used in daily practice. Most of these instruments work according to the *magnetostrictive* or reciprocal *piëzo-electric* principle. These instruments are mainly applied to the treatment of periodontal disease, but there are also applications within the field of endodontics and restorative dentistry.

In 1955, Zinner looked for alternative applications and introduced the ultrasonic instrument into periodontal therapy. He showed that the ultrasonic tips could be used for removing calculus (without the abrasive paste). This caused a revolution in the treatment of periodontal diseases. At first, application was mainly limited to the supragingival area. In the 1960s, Dr Thomas Holbrook introduced the first modified tip (P-10) and developed a technique with which subgingival debridement could be carried out almost exclusively with ultrasonic scalers. In the 1980s, it appeared that hand and ultrasonic instrumentation, as far as healing is concerned, produce similar results both after initial periodontal treatment and also during maintenance. Fifty years after the introduction of ultrasonic instruments, the effects these tools have on the teeth and the periodontium have become much clearer. Additionally, there are new and modified tips as well as improved instrumentation techniques. Moreover, routine use of ultrasonic instruments reduces the need to use a vast assortment of hand instruments. Frequently a complete professional dental prophylaxis can be performed with one universal tip when treating patients with gingivitis and also for routine periodontal maintenance.
A marked ergonomic advantage is the reduced need to constantly reach for the instrument tray. Furthermore, the tips do not have to be sharpened. However it must be remembered that, in certain patients, pocket anatomy will require the use of hand instruments which have shafts with multiple angles and should be easily available.

This monograph presents the mechanism, scientific basis, and correct use of ultrasonic instruments and offers the reader key insights for their successful use.

Fig 2
Mechanical scalers (left to right). The sonic scaler (Kavo Sonicflex) and the piëzo-electric ultrasonic scalers (EMS & Satelec).

MECHANICAL SCALERS

In periodontal practice, increasing use is made of electric and air-operated mechanical scalers (Fig 2 and Table 1) in addition to hand instruments. The first development within dentistry was the ultrasonic scaler. When initially introduced, these instruments were intended to be a fast and effective aid in cases in which large quantities of calculus formed on tooth surfaces. In general, large thick tips were solely available, thus cleaning primarily the supragingival surfaces of the teeth. These tips provided little tactile feeling and made it difficult to perform adequate subgingival debridement. Scaling with these instruments frequently resulted in a rough root surface. Consequently, hand instruments were necessary to correct this problem. Present-day instruments use thinner and longer (slimmer) straight tips with the result that the area of the tooth surface accessible to the ultrasonic scaler has been markedly extended. It is now easier to gain access to the subgingival area, making it possible to remove plaque and calculus from these difficult-to-reach areas.

Energy in the form of ultrasonic waves is transferred to the gingiva, enamel, dentine, root canal, and pulp. A part of this energy is converted into heat, which can lead to a temperature rise of the dental and periodontal tissues. For this reason an efficient cooling system is needed to regulate the temperature change. Water, which functions as a coolant, is transferred to the end of the ultrasonic tip and in addition creates a fine spray. A further advantage is that the spray helps to wash away the loosened plaque and calculus. The liquid not only functions as a coolant but also contributes to the general efficacy of the scaler through the "cavitation effect" that occurs in the liquid. If the ultrasonic instrument is used correctly, it can function perfectly as a replacement for hand instruments, and, according to Leon & Vogel (1987), it has become the primary choice in furcation areas.

Table 1 Various types of mechanical scalers and their modes of action:

Sonic	> Vibration generated by an air turbine in the handpiece.
	> The movement of the tip is mainly circular.
	> 2,500 to 16,000 Hz.
	> Example: Sonicflex/Kavo.
Ultrasonic magneto-strictive	> Flat metal strips or a ferro-magnetic bar is attached to the tip.
	> There is a spiral of copper wire in the handpiece, which creates a magnetic field on passing a current through the device.
	> The movement of the tip is mainly elliptic.
	> 18,000 to 45,000 Hz.
	> Examples: Cavitron SPS/Dentsply, Odontson-M/Goof.
Ultrasonic piëzo-electric	> Electrically reactive quartz crystals in the handle create dimensional changes (shrinkage & elongation) when an alternating current passes through the device.
	> These dimensional changes are transmitted to the tip.
	> The movement of the tip is mainly linear.
	> 25,000 to 50,000 Hz.
	> Examples: Piëzon master/EMS, P-max/Satelec.

EFFECTS OF THE SONIC SCALER

In addition to ultrasonic instruments, there are also sonic instruments (Fig 3) or air scalers available on the market. Sonic scalers are, in fact, air turbines, which work on the air pressure of the dental unit. A major advantage is that they can be easily connected to the multiflex attachment of the unit. However, they make a great deal of noise and produce a high whistling sound. The frequency of the vibrations is much lower than that of ultrasonic scalers.

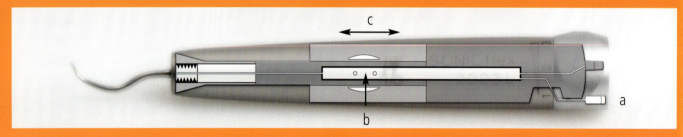

Fig 3a Schematic cross section of a sonic handpiece (a = tube for air supply, b = angulated holes in the air tube, c = tube can slide back and forth).

The vibrations are not generated by electricity but by compressed air driven through the handle. The way in which this occurs depends on the mechanism of the internal components. This results in a vibration frequency of the tip of approximately 2,500 to 16,000 Hz. The point of the tip makes a movement with a deflection of 0.08 to 0.2 mm. The greatest deflection of the tip is peri-axial. Because of the lower vibration frequency, the efficiency of the tip is also less than that of ultrasonic instruments.

Fig 3b Sonicflex handpiece (Kavo) with a set of perio-tips.

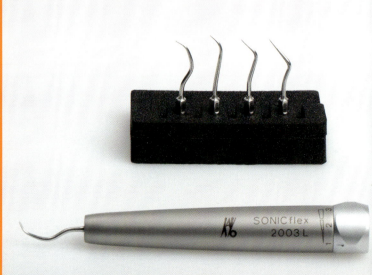

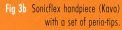

However, a sonic scaler appears to be effective in the removal of plaque. This is probably due to the more elliptic/circular movement of the tip of the scaler (Fig 4). The effectiveness of the tip is greatly reduced when considerable pressure is placed on it. Unfortunately, this does not involve a reduction of the noise produced by the handpiece; thus, the operator is not directly aware of a decrease in the effectiveness of the tip. The internal part of the handle consists of a hollow tube and a rotor. The scaler tips are screwed onto the handpiece and connected to the tube in this way. There are many types of tips which are generally blunt and are similar to an ultra-sonic scaler. Fig 3a shows a schematic view of a sonic handpiece. The air being supplied is transferred by means of a tube (a) through the angulated holes (b). The tube will start to tilt (c), resulting in the tube hitting against the vibratory pipe. Ultimately this generates the vibrations. The vibrations are transferred to the tip via the vibra-tory pipe (Fig 5), but are also simultaneously being cushioned by a rubber ring. No heat is developed in the handle. However, water cooling is needed in order to reduce the amount of frictional heat the tip produces on the tooth surface.

(Sonic equipment is not explicitly addressed in this monograph. The emphasis will be on ultrasonic instrumentation since most of the research has focused on this group of instruments.)

Sonic Ultrasonic Piëzo-electric Ultrasonic Magneto-strictive

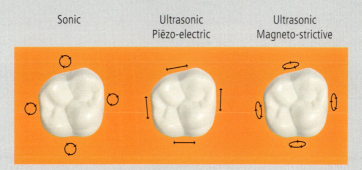

Fig 4 Movement of the sonic, piëzo-electric, and magneto-strictive tips. *(Left)* The sonic scaler makes a circular movement. *(Middle)* A piëzo-electric ultrasonic scaler mainly moves linearly. *(Right)* A magneto-strictive ultrasonic scaler makes an elliptic movement. Modified after Petersilka & Flemmig, 1999.

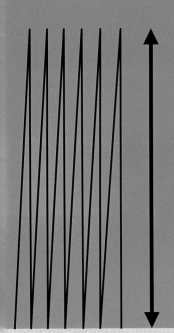
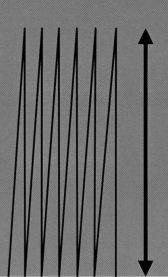

Fig 5 Amplitude is the distance the tip moves.

EFFECTS OF THE ULTRASONIC SCALER

Ultrasonic waves are the mechanical transference of energy via a suitable medium. The waves are created when particles are charged with energy, which makes them vibrate and transfer energy to adjoining particles. The energy is conducted in a wave form. When an ultrasonic wave encounters an interface between two different media such as dental tissues, a part is reflected back into the original medium. The remaining energy continues on into the new medium. The amount that is reflected back is called *acoustic impedance*. A greater energy transfer takes place between media if the impedance is similar. Large impedance differences exist between solid materials, fluids, and gases, allowing little energy transfer.

Ultrasonic instruments are based on the principle that electric energy in the form of rapid vibrations varying from 18,000 to 50,000 Hz (vibrations per second) is converted into mechanical energy. Ultrasonic vibrations are made up of waves, which:
- Move longitudinally;
- Must have matter as a medium for transfer;
- Are reflected and absorbed at the interface of different tissues.

Although there are many brands of ultrasonic units and tips, there are only two basic types: magneto-strictive or piëzo-electric (see Table 1 on page 11).

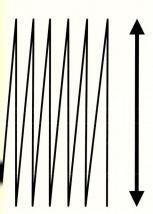

The ultrasonic unit consists of an electric generator, a handpiece which holds several interchangeable tips, and a foot switch. The electric generator converts the electric current into a high-frequency vibration. When the foot switch is engaged, the electric current is sent to the handle by the generator (unit). The handle holds the transducer, which converts the electric energy into mechanical vibrations. With both types of apparatus mentioned previously, it is possible to regulate the water supply, and it is also possible to regulate the amplitude of the vibrations (the distance across which the tip moves) by means of the "power" button (Fig 5). The vibrations are not visible to the naked eye and vary in amplitude from 0.006 to 0.1 mm. The amplitude depends on the power setting, the flexibility of the metal, the cooling fluid supply, and the length of the tip. If the amplitude increases, the energy and, consequently, the efficiency of the tip increase. With subgingival instrumentation the power can be reduced in order to cause as little damage as possible in this restricted area.

Some magneto-strictive units also have a "tuning" button with which the frequency of the vibrations can be regulated. The frequency is the number of times per second the tip moves back and forth and partially determines the speed of the tip (speed/displacement = frequency × amplitude × time). Most ultrasonic units are *auto tuned*, however, which makes it impossible to regulate the frequency. The frequency is raised automatically as the power is reduced.

Magneto-strictive unit

The magneto-strictive effect was discovered by James Prescott Joule in 1842. He noticed that within a magnetic field certain ferro-magnetic materials, such as iron and nickel, had the ability to change in length. The characteristic component of the magneto-strictive unit (Fig 6) is the pack of thin metal strips (nickel-cobalt) that have been soldered together at the ends, or a ferro-magnetic bar (ferrite). The metal strips/bar are attached to the tip (ie, insert) and resemble a tuning fork in their mode of action. This ultrasonic insert is slid into the handle which contains a spiral of copper wire. This spiral generates a magnetic field from the moment the current starts to flow. The combination of several metals reacts harmoniously to the changing electric fields.

Fig 6 Schematic cross section of the magneto-strictive handpiece.

The pack of metal strips or the bar then contracts. An alternating current produces a changing magnetic field. If the magnetic field alternates (turned "on" and "off"), the pack of strips or the bar changes form continuously, and, perpendicular to the longitudinal axis, vibrations are generated. This occurs with a frequency of twice that of the change taking place in the magnetic field. These changes in dimension are transmitted to the tip, which starts vibrating, thereby creating a form of elliptic spiral movement (see Fig 4). This particular movement of the magneto-strictive tip ensures the simultaneous activity of all surfaces of the tip, allowing the side, back, or front of the tip to be used on the tooth surface. All sides of the tip are effective. Magneto-strictive scalers move at a frequency between 18,000 and 45,000 Hz. The water flowing through the handpiece has a threefold purpose:

- It ensures the cooling of the metal strips in the handpiece;
- It cools the tooth surface that is being cleaned;
- It helps to wash away calculus particles and plaque deposits during the treatment.

Piëzo-electric unit

In 1880, Pierre & Jacques Curie described the piëzo-electric effect. This is the generation of electricity when quartz crystals are placed under pressure. When a tensile force is applied to the crystals, the polarity of the current reverses. The term *piëzo-electricity* finds its origin in the Greek word *piezin* which means "pressure." Piëzo-electricity can be observed through many naturally occurring crystals, such as quartz and tourmaline. The effect can be reversed when the crystal is placed in an electric field; then a crystal will start vibrating with a frequency dependent on the alternating current (Fig 7). The piëzo-electric dental unit works according to this principle, except in reverse—the so-called reciprocal effect (see Fig 7). A number of electrically reactive ceramic disks are embedded in the instrument handle. If the electric current alternates, this causes a change of shape (contraction and elongation), which is transmitted to the tip. No magnetic field is present.

Fig 7 The working mode of a piëzo-electric element.

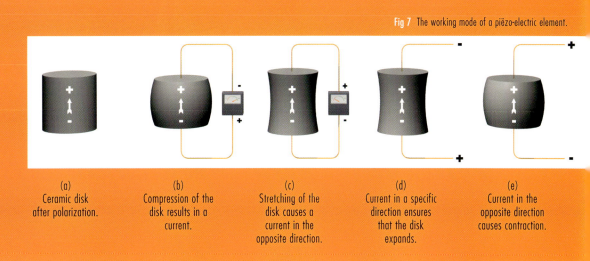

(a)	(b)	(c)	(d)	(e)
Ceramic disk after polarization.	Compression of the disk results in a current.	Stretching of the disk causes a current in the opposite direction.	Current in a specific direction ensures that the disk expands.	Current in the opposite direction causes contraction.

Figure 8a shows a schematic cross section of the piëzo element in an ultrasonic handpiece. The element contains four crystal disks which, by means of contact plates, allow the passage of an electric current. By alternating the electric current, the crystals will expand and contract, thereby creating the vibration frequency. The total expansion of the four disks determines the length of deflection of the tip. The crystal disks are embedded in the handle and envelop a metal bar which has a contra-weight at one end. The other end of the metal bar has a screw thread on which a scaler tip can be attached. Figures 8b and 8c show two piezo-electric units.

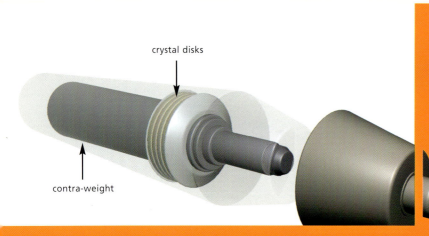

crystal disks

contra-weight

Fig 8a Schematic cross section of the piëzo-electric handpiece.

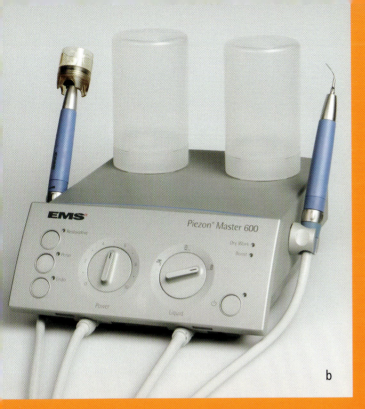

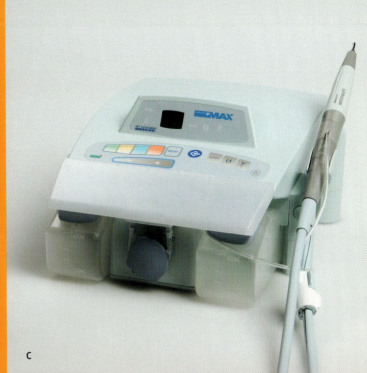

b

c

Figs 8b and 8c Modern piëzo-electric units: (left) Piëzon master (EMS) and (right) P-max (Satelec).

A special torque-control key to place the tip with the correct amount of force prevents damage to the threads (Fig 9). The direction of the vibration is longitudinal relative to the handle of the handpiece. This results in a linear back-and-forth movement of the tip (see Fig 4). Consequently, both sides of the tip are effective. A piëzo-electric scaler moves with a frequency between 25,000 and 50,000 Hz. The cooling ensures that the temperature at the tip is regulated. This is mandatory, since frictional energy from instrumentation will cause a temperature rise at both the tip and tooth surface.

Fig 9 Torque-control keys of the Kavo Sonicflex, EMS, and Satelec.

COOLING SCALER TIPS

The ultrasonic vibratory waves move through the tissues while the energy of these waves decreases and is partially converted into heat. This will result in a rise in temperature of the tooth surface and surrounding tissues. The effect on the tissues is dependent on the degree of the temperature increase, its duration, and the sensitivity of the tissue. In most tissues the normal physiological response is to raise the blood flow, which will help to regulate the temperature.

In addition, a good cooling system is needed to regulate the temperature. As stated previously, a magneto-strictive unit needs cooling not only for the ultrasonic tip, but also for the pack of metal strips/bar. As the coolant flows from the handpiece to the tip, it becomes warmed. With insufficient water supply, the cooling will be inadequate and the temperature of the water will rise. The operator can test the temperature of the water flow on the wrist. In contrast, the piëzo-electric units and sonic scalers only need the tips to be cooled. Consequently, less coolant is needed.

The stream of water serves as a coolant to counteract the development of frictional heat and also to prevent pain or even damage to the pulp. Moreover, the vibrating tip generates a water spray. This ensures not only a constant washing of the pocket during instrumentation, but a "cavitation" may also occur, which contributes to the cleaning of the tooth and root surface. Another advantage of the coolant is that the work field is continuously flushed, which ensures good visibility for the operator.

Fig 10
Cavitation effect (cavitation bubbles) and micro-streaming, which occur when an activated ultrasonic tip is immersed into a liquid.

Cavitation

A unique characteristic of the ultrasonic scalers is the cavitation effect and the micro-streaming that occurs in the cooling liquid. Micro-streaming is the result of the rapid movement of the ultrasonic scaler, leading to turbulence around its tip (Fig 10). During ultrasonic instrumentation the coolant is under the influence of the rapidly alternating tensile and compressive forces, which pulls the fluid apart. This causes marked local reductions in pressure. When the pressure is reduced to the level at which vaporization occurs, small hollows resembling bubbles are formed at the end of the ultrasonic tip, where the maximum vibration occurs. These bubbles are filled with water vapor/gas and vibrate along with their source. These bubbles grow and finally become so large that they can no longer keep pace with the vibrations. This will cause them to implode and form a mass of micro-bubbles and may lead to shock waves. This phenomenon is called *cavitation* (Fig 11) and depends on the frequency, not the amplitude, of the ultrasonic vibration.

Ultrasonic effect in the water coolant

When the cooling liquid is transferred to the vibrating tip, two hydrodynamic effects may occur: (1) cavitation and (2) acoustic micro-streaming. If ultrasonic energy of more than one third watt per cm^2 is applied to a liquid medium, cavitation occurs. This is the result of the fast movement of a solid metal tip in a liquid. This results in small cavitation bubbles (Fig 11a). These bubbles develop and implode in the areas of the tip where it vibrates at the maximum speed (Fig 11b). A great deal of energy is locally released due to the implosion, leading to a local rise in temperature and pressure. This temperature and pressure wave is capable of rupturing bacterial cell walls. Prof A.D. Walmsley has conducted a great deal of research studying the effects of ultrasonics and has looked at the effect of cavitation on a surface covered with plaque. Figure 12 shows that if only the mechanical effect of the tip is used, only a small area of the surface is cleaned. This area increases when adding the coolant.

Acoustic micro-streaming is a simpler process. In the liquid, a vortex-like situation is created (Fig 11c), which is generated by the powerful ultrasonic vibrations and the small space in which the tip can move. This has no bactericidal effect, but it helps to remove the plaque from the tooth's surface and to flush out the pocket (or the root canals during endodontic treatment). Both effects contribute to a better cleaning of a tooth surface covered with plaque (in some studies even 500% more), but are not specific to ultrasonic instruments and can also be observed when sonic instruments are used.

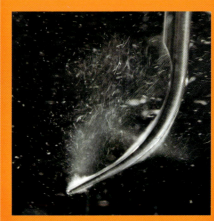

Fig 11a

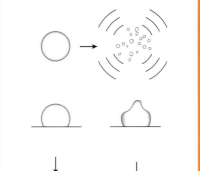

Fig 11b
Modified after Laird & Walmsley, 1991.

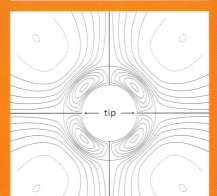

Fig 11c
Modified after Laird & Walmsley, 1991.

The implosion of the cavitation bubbles signifies an abrupt change from the gas/vapor phase to the liquid phase, which can result in high molecular forces being released. Theoretically, the pressure can rise to a couple of hundred or thousand bars and the temperature can rise to approximately 2,700°C. Thus the surface is exposed to mechanical, thermal, and electrophysical forces, which lead to an erosive effect.

In *Webster's* dictionary, *cavitation* is described as the formation of vapor cavities in the water flowing around the blades of a propeller due to excessive speed of rotation, resulting in structural damage or a loss of efficiency. The extent to which this cavitation effect contributes to the removal of plaque (biofilm), calculus, and the release of endotoxins from the root surface has not been determined.

In the 1950s research workers were under the impression that direct contact between the tip and the root surface was not necessary for the cleaning effect. Shortly thereafter, this suggestion was refuted when it became clear that the cavitation effect is inadequate to remove calculus. However, it has been shown that cavitation is capable of removing firmly attached matter, such as plaque, from hard surfaces. This takes place up to approximately 0.5 mm from the point of the tip (see Fig 12). The quantity of plaque that is removed depends on the type of tip used and the placement of the tip with regard to the tooth surface. The cleaning effect of cavitation is not the result of a single bubble, but the combined effect of thousands of bubbles.

With ultrasonic scalers, an acoustic field of micro-streaming occurs around the tip. The forces that are released are large enough to cause damage to platelets. In the presence of blood, the cavitation effect can also result in a thrombogenic effect: the lysis of erythrocytes and platelets. This may explain the reduction in hemorrhage that occurs with ultrasonic scalers.

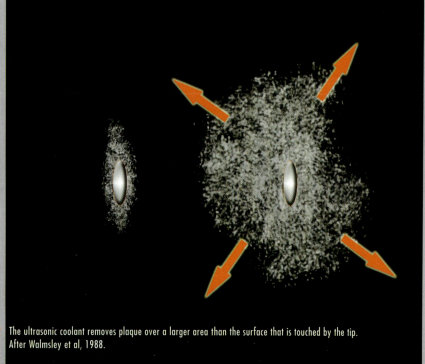

Fig 12 The ultrasonic coolant removes plaque over a larger area than the surface that is touched by the tip.
After Walmsley et al, 1988.

Aerosol

During the use of ultrasonic instruments, an *aerosol* is created, which literally means a dispersion of very fine particles (< 100 μm). A *dental aerosol* is defined as a cloud comprised of millions of very small water particles, which are dispersed with great speed through, for example, a handpiece, multi-functional syringe, or mechanical scaler. Aerosol particles appear in both solid and liquid forms. The solid particles consist mainly of dentine, enamel, and calculus. The liquid droplets are primarily cooling fluid and saliva, and are also loaded with microorganisms from plaque. Blood has also been found in the aerosol, even if it is not visible.

The occurrence of pathogenic aerosols is of importance for patients, assistants, and dental professionals. Effective infection control is mandatory at all times. This is true not only during but also after treatment. An aerosol remains in the air for more than 30 minutes. For the operator, a face mask and protective glasses offer the needed protection against the larger particles. A face mask that filters to a high degree and adapts well to the face markedly reduces the risk of infection. If the face mask becomes moist during the treatment it should be replaced every 30 minutes in order to prevent the penetration of moisture.

Caution is needed for patients with a reduced resistance against bacterial infections: In these specific cases, the bacterially charged aerosol could increase the risk of illness. A face mask covering the nose might offer protection for these patients. The hepatitis virus and HIV have been detected in saliva and blood and thus may also occur in the aerosol. The risk of infection with the hepatitis virus by means of aerosol is small but potentially present. HIV is not as easily transferred; the risk of infection via an aerosol is considered small, even unlikely, but cannot be excluded. For this reason and wherever possible, preventive measures must be taken. However, it must be understood that there is absolutely no proof that either an operator or patient has yet presented with a serious illness caused by an aerosol.

With simple measures a considerable reduction of aerosol can be achieved. Frequently quoted research from 1967 reports that the number of bacteria in the air increases during and after the use of ultrasonic instruments, up to 30 times the level found before the treatment. This investigation was conducted in an era when there were only low volume aspirators. More recent in vitro research shows that an aspirator placed around the ultrasonic handpiece reduced the aerosol by 93%. Recent in vivo research has shown that the use of modern high-volume aspirators offers good protection against bacterial aerosol during the use of piëzo-electric ultrasonic instruments (Timmerman et al, 2004). It should be emphasized for both the operator and assistant that the aspirator should not be held close to the tip of the mechanical scaler, since this may lead to a risk of inadequate cooling.

Additional protection can be obtained by having the patient rinse with antimicrobial rinsing agents (preferably chlorhexidine) before the treatment with mechanical scalers. This could possibly reduce the bacterially charged aerosol. This rinsing prior to treatment appears to result in a major reduction of the number of bacteria in the saliva. Studies have shown that rinsing 60 seconds with chlorhexidine before treatment will reduce the bacterial load in the saliva by approximately 90%, and this effect lasts for ± 60 minutes during subgingival instrumentation.

This simple, practical approach is therefore recommended. It has also been shown that if the area is rinsed with a phenol-containing mouthwash (for instance, Listerine) for 30 seconds prior to the treatment, the number of viable bacteria in an aerosol decreases by ≅ 94%. The guidelines of the American Dental Association state that a clean white coat has to be worn every day since an operator's uniform readily becomes fouled by the aerosol.

Antimicrobial liquid coolant

A common concern is that insufficient cooling of the tip would take place during subgingival instrumentation. Studies by Nosal (1991) have shown that with the movements of the tip, the water reaches the total depth of the pocket. It appears that the vibration of the tip projects the stream of water into the pocket and the point of the tip is therefore sufficiently cooled. As the pocket is irrigated to its maximum depth, an antimicrobial agent added to the coolant would possibly provide an extra, favorable effect. However, it should be pointed out that the coolant does not penetrate further than the path taken by instrumentation with the tip. Thus, in order to reach the entire subgingival area with the liquid coolant, it is important to instrument thoroughly, allowing all of the recesses of the pocket to be reached by the tip.

The clinical advantages of the use of ultrasonic scalers with an antimicrobial coolant instead of just plain tap water have not been well documented. A number of short-term studies examined a solution of 0.02% and of 0.12% chlorhexidine (CHX) and discovered no additional clinical effect. Other research observed that the CHX group in comparison to regular tap water showed a significantly greater reduction in pockets that were 4 to 6 mm initially. With the cooling of 0.12% CHX, an additional 0.5 mm pocket depth reduction was reached. The question remains whether this limited benefit justifies the use of a relatively expensive antimicrobial rinsing agent. A number of studies have examined the effect of antimicrobials added to the coolant in order to assess whether or not an additional improvement could be achieved in the clinical result. However, there is no current research showing that this addition to the coolant would reduce the aerosol effect.

In certain cases, there is a renewed interest in the use of an antimicrobial coolant when specific antimicrobial therapies are indicated. For instance, this could have an added value in immunocompromised patients, or patients with an advanced, recurrent/refractory periodontitis.

Various small clinical studies have shown that the effect of professional debridement is enhanced if iodine is locally applied. Iodine could therefore be part of a potential antimicrobial coolant. However, this needs to be confirmed in larger, controlled clinical studies. Moreover, there is a serious risk of hypersensitivity when using iodine (eg, iodine allergy, cross allergy for shellfish). Iodine also is hazardous to the fetus. In the United States, the use of iodine has been reported as contraindicated in women who may become pregnant.

EFFECTS OF PROFESSIONAL SUPRA- AND SUBGINGIVAL DEBRIDEMENT

In many studies the effectiveness of professional debridement is related to the ability to remove plaque, calculus, and endotoxins (bacterial products) and to the degree of smoothness of the treated tooth surfaces. After reviewing the various studies, the limitations of every analysis method should be taken into account. Additionally, the type of instrument, the tooth type, the anatomy of the root, the initial pocket depth, the patient's cooperation, and in particular the manual skills of the operator may have an effect on the outcome of the results. This hampers the comparability between the studies.

Clinical results of manual instruments versus mechanical scalers

When mechanical scalers or hand instruments are used for supra- and subgingival debridement, the clinical results (pocket depth, attachment level, and bleeding tendency) are not significantly different (Table 2).

Table 2 The clinical effect of hand instruments and mechanical scalers

Reference	Instruments	Probing depth		SC/PL per tooth (min)	Study length (mo)
		Before SC/PL	Reduction after SC/PL		
Torfason et al, 1979 (n = 18)	Hand Ultrasonic	5.0 mm	1.70 mm	3.8 3.0	2
Badersten et al, 1981 (n = 16)	Hand Ultrasonic	4.2 mm	1.30 mm	NA	8
Badersten et al, 1985 (n = 16)	Hand Ultrasonic	5.5 mm	1.90 mm	10.7	12
Boretti et al, 1995 (n = 19)	Hand Ultrasonic	5.74 mm 6.04 mm	1.83 mm 1.82 mm	8.5 4.3	1
Laurell et al, 1988 (n = 12)	Hand Sonic	NA	72%• 67%•	12 NA	4 8
Laurell, 1990 (n = 16)	Sonic	NA	80%	NA	8
Loos et al, 1987 (n = 12)	Sonic or Ultrasonic	≤ 3.5 mm 4–6.5 mm ≥ 7 mm	0.00 mm 1.30 mm 2.70 mm		12
Loos et al, 1989 (n = 12)	Sonic or Ultrasonic	≤ 3.5 mm 4–6.5 mm ≥ 7 mm	−0.50 mm 1.20 mm 2.30 mm	6.7 (molars) 3.7 (others)	24

SC = scaling; PL = planing.

• Percent reduction of the number of pockets ≥ 4 mm as compared to baseline.

In a number of short-term studies (eg, Torfason, 1979), a comparable pocket depth reduction and decrease of bleeding occurs within a period of 3 to 8 weeks following treatment. Also, the long-term clinical results show no significant difference between both instrumentation methods. Badersten et al evaluated the clinical effect of professional debridement in several classic studies. In their first publication (1981), they compared the two instrumentation methods in adult periodontitis patients (average initial probing depth 4.1 to 4.5 mm). After the patients had been taught adequate oral hygiene, the incisors, canines, and premolars were professionally cleaned with hand or ultrasonic instruments according to a split-mouth research protocol. The clinical results (plaque, bleeding, and probing pocket depth) of the treatment were evaluated every 3 months. Three months after professional debridement, a reduction in bleeding on probing could be observed. Only 14% to 18% of the measured pockets still showed bleeding on probing, while the initial bleeding tendency was 90%. The mean initial probing depth after the treatment dropped between 1.3 mm and 1.7 mm in 4 to 5 months. Reduction appeared to be greatest in pockets with a large initial probing depth. These clinical results remained stable through the end of the study period (2 years). In their follow-up research (Badersten et al, 1984), they looked into the effect of the professional debridement in patients with *severe advanced* adult periodontitis (average initial probing depth 5.5 mm to 5.8 mm). Three months after scaling, they observed a reduction in bleeding on probing similar to their previous work. Within 12 months following treatment, the average initial probing pocket depth had dropped to a mean of 3.6 mm to 3.9 mm. The clinical improvement remained stable through the end of the study period (2 years). There was no difference between the two operators. The study of Ruhling (2002) has shown that the operator's skill and experience affect the results of professional debridement. It was also observed that a trained operator was able to treat a far greater area during a treatment session than an untrained operator.

Changes in clinical attachment level were not examined in most of these clinical studies. Nevertheless, if the previous studies are taken into account, it can be assumed that the attachment level will show similar improvement. It is still unclear to what extent the tip movement or frequency of the mechanical instrumentation will affect the clinical efficacy, as well as how the various instruments will affect the root surface. The instruments differ in range of frequency (2,500 to 50,000 Hz) and the direction of the tip movement (linear, elliptic, circular). In spite of this, studies comparing sonic, piëzo-electric, and magneto-strictive scalers show almost the same clinical results.

For this reason, hand instruments and mechanical scalers, either used in combination or alone, appear to be suitable for the mechanical cleaning of periodontal pockets and able to achieve the desired therapeutic goals. The improvement of the clinical parameters is nearly equal for all instrumentation methods, as long as sufficient time is spent on thoroughly cleaning the root surfaces. Two recent systematic reviews (Hallmon & Rees, 2003; Tunkel et al, 2002) support this conclusion.

Removal of plaque (biofilm)

Research has shown that there is no difference in the effectiveness of plaque removal using hand or mechanical instruments. Neither method of instrumentation will completely remove all microbial plaque and calculus deposits; this has been shown with studies on extracted teeth. The remaining plaque and calculus on these treated teeth were assessed after the root surfaces were treated with disclosing solution. Frequently, 10% to 30% of the treated surface was still covered with plaque. This plaque was primarily found in the apical portion of the pocket. The deeper the pocket, the more difficult it seemed for both instruments to remove the adhered plaque. Compared to hand instrumentation, ultrasonic instruments have the advantage of removing plaque faster. A time savings of 20% to 50% has been reported.

An effective subgingival plaque control is needed for optimal periodontal healing and maintenance of a healthy periodontium over a long-term period. Removal of subgingival plaque is important because recolonization will take place within a few months in spite of good supragingival plaque control, and even within a few weeks with poor plaque control. The recolonization of bacteria is the basic reason for the dentist and/or dental hygienist to perform professional mechanical subgingival debridement over and over again at frequent intervals. The use of slim ultrasonic tips at a lower power setting makes ultrasonic instruments particularly suitable for use during periodic periodontal maintenance. By using the ultrasonic instruments in this manner, the plaque (biofilm) can be easily removed both from tooth surfaces and within the pockets with minimal risk of damage to the tooth and the surrounding tissues. Additional treatment with hand instruments during maintenance care may not be necessary, allowing extra time for instructing and training the patient in adequate self-care (oral hygiene).

Effect on the composition of the microflora

When the severity of the periodontal inflammation increases, a shift in the composition of the subgingival microflora occurs. The microflora, which in a healthy situation contains primarily gram-positive facultative anaeobic microorganisms, becomes populated primarily with gram-negative anaerobic microorganisms. As is commonly accepted, disruption and reduction of the supra- and subgingival microflora are important for obtaining a successful treatment result. Professional supra- and subgingival debridement significantly reduces gram-negative bacteria, motile rods, and spirochetes and increases the number of gram-positive cocci. Moreover, a reduction in the total number of colony-forming bacteria occurs after treatment.

Due to the cavitation effect, substantial forces are produced locally that erode and remove plaque, and a great deal of energy is released locally, resulting in high temperatures and increased pressure (see Fig 11). Because of the increased temperature and the pressure wave, the bacterial cell wall may break. The literature has examined whether such an antibacterial effect is measurable. To achieve this, the composition of the subgingival microflora was compared following treatment with mechanical scalers and hand instruments. The reduction in subgingival microflora did not show a considerable difference between techniques.

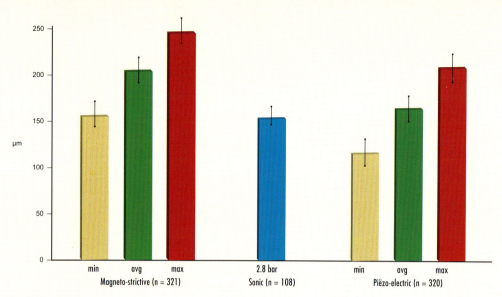

Fig 13 Cumulative loss of dental tissue through instrumentation with mechanical scalers dependent on the adjusted power setting. Based on data from Petersilka & Flemmig, 1999.

Removal of calculus

Calculus is a rough, porous substance that attaches to the root surface and enhances plaque retention. The objective of professional debridement is to remove the deposits of calculus as effectively as possible. Care has to be taken to cause little or no damage to the surface of the tooth. Complete calculus removal requires extensive instrumentation, which can also result in a significant amount of damage to the enamel, dentine, and/or root cementum. This could lead to hypersensitivity of the teeth and even pulpitis in more severe cases. Loss of dental tissue will increase exponentially when the "power" is increased from average to high (Fig 13). Therefore, it is preferable to avoid using the ultrasonic scaler at the highest power setting. Studies show that extensive iatrogenic damage to the root surface during treatment can be prevented when the number of slightly overlapping movements with the mechanical scaler are limited to a minimum. The tip should be placed against the surface with light pressure (Fig 14). Subsequently, back and forth "sweeping" movements are made in such a way that the pattern of vibration is parallel to the tooth/root surface. Use of the tip at an angle between 0 and 15 degrees in relation to the root surface makes it possible for the operator to obtain complete removal of the calculus without causing excessive damage to the root surfaces (Fig 14).

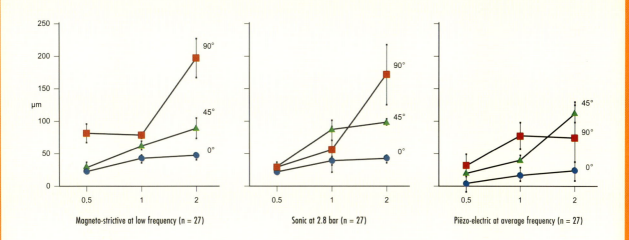

Fig 14 The angle of the tip in relation to the tooth surface and the pressure of the tip on the surface (measured in newtons), in relationship to the depth of the defect after instrumentation. *(Left)* Magneto-strictive ultrasonic scaler used at low frequency. *(Middle)* Sonic scaler at 2.8 bar. *(Right)* Piëzo-electric ultrasonic scaler used at the average frequency. Based on data from Petersilka & Flemmig, 1999.

Removal of endotoxins and root cementum

The objective of scaling is to remove plaque, calculus, and stain from the crown and root surfaces. This is in contrast to root planing, which is the definitive removal of cementum or dentine from the root surface in an attempt to smooth rough surfaces, remove soft and/or necrotic cementum, eliminate bacteria, reduce impregnated toxins (endotoxins), and dislodge calculus. According to some researchers, the success of professional debridement is based upon the successful removal of endotoxins from the root surfaces. These endotoxins are cell wall fragments and toxic (waste) products of bacteria and can be found in the radicular cementum/dentine, the saliva, and the crevicular fluid. Significantly higher concentrations of endotoxins are found on the root surfaces of periodontally affected teeth. As the clinical symptoms of periodontal inflammation become more severe, the amount of endotoxins in the crevicular fluid also increases. Endotoxins are cytotoxic and can affect the host immune system. It is suggested that for treatment to succeed, the contaminated dentine and the "diseased" cementum have to be removed. Until recently, it was accepted that endotoxins were strongly attached and imbedded into the radicular cementum/dentine. In order to remove these endotoxins, planing of the root surface—an intensive removal of the root cementum—was thought to be necessary.

Recent studies show that after the use of both hand instruments and mechanical scalers, the endotoxin count drops to a level that is normally found around healthy teeth. These endotoxins are probably superficially connected to the radicular dentine and cementum. Therefore these bacterial products are easily removed by rinsing, brushing, lightly scaling, or polishing the root surface. Intentional removal of radicular cementum is no longer deemed necessary to achieve periodontal healing, and the removal of toxic substances from the root surface is not felt to be mandatory (Smart et al, 1990).

Is the apical part of the pocket reached?

Adequate cleaning of a deep inflamed pocket presents a challenge to the operator and becomes more difficult as the pocket becomes deeper. In pockets ≥ 4 mm, the use of hand instruments for complete removal of subgingival plaque and calculus has been shown to be unfeasible (Rateitschak-Pluss et al, 1992). Research by Dragoo (1992) with a thin, modified ultrasonic tip showed that the base of the pocket was reached more satisfactorily with this slim ultrasonic tip. However, his research revealed that complete removal of the

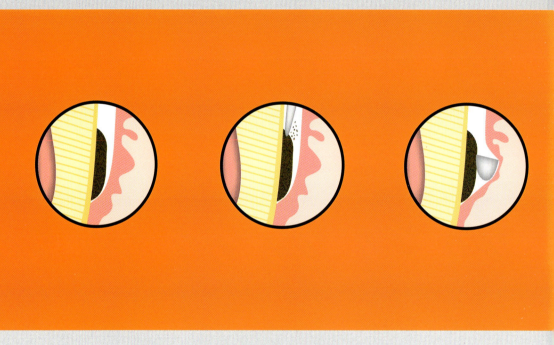

Fig 15 The curette has to be placed more apically than the calculus deposit to remove it from the root surface. Each movement and contact over subgingival calculus can be considered an active stroke because the ultrasonic tip continuously vibrates.

subgingival plaque and calculus from deeper pockets (6 to 8 mm) with either hand or ultrasonic instruments was an unobtainable goal.

Figure 15 shows an "artist's impression" of why the base of the pocket is more easily accessed and adequately cleaned with the use of an ultrasonic tip. The curette has to be placed apical to the calculus deposit in order to remove it with an active stroke. Close to the base of the pocket, the curette often experiences resistance arising in the connective tissue and the alveolar bone. Under these circumstances, the ultrasonic instrument is superior, since the calculus can be removed by approaching it coronally. Each movement and contact over subgingival calculus can be considered an active stroke because the tip continuously vibrates.

Access to furcations

Hand instruments are inadequate to remove attached plaque and calculus from furcations. Studies have shown that this applies to situations where the furcations are instrumented without direct vision as well as during flap surgery, when visibility should be optimal. If the furcations are only slightly accessible (Class I), it appears that hand instruments and mechanical scalers are equally effective. Ultrasonic tips seem to provide a clear advantage in furcations that are more accessible (Class II & III).

Ultrasonic tips, when used well, can be considered a good replacement for hand instruments, and they are the first choice in furcation areas according to Leon & Vogel (1987). Most furcation entrances are much narrower than the average width of the working blade of a curette. For example, the access to the buccal furcation at the site of the first and second maxillary molar varies in width, on average, between 0.63 and 1.04 mm. For mandibular molars, this value is 0.71 to 0.88 mm. The width of a new Gracey curette measures between 0.76 and 1.00 mm (Fig 16). It is almost certain that the infected furcation area in second molars cannot be approached with a curette. In such instances, the slim tips of the ultrasonic instrument with a diameter of 0.55 mm should simplify access. There are also tips that are shaped similarly to a furcation probe, which make furcations even more accessible (Fig 17). In addition, EMS manufactures tips that are curved similar to a furcation probe and also with a small sphere (Ø 0.8 mm) at the end (Fig 18).

It is thought that this small sphere provides more surface area at the end of the tip, which makes it especially suited for cleaning furcations and concavities. Schroer et al (1991) described furcation problems that were treated with open (surgical) curettage. These lost on average 0.46 mm clinical attachment whereas in the control sites, which were treated with conventional subgingival debridement, a clinical attachment gain of approximately 0.5 mm was realized.

Fig 16 The part of the curette blade that was measured.

Fig 17 Ultrasonic tips (Satelec: TU2-IL, TU2-1R) that have the shape of a furcation probe facilitate access to the furcation.

Fig 18 Ultrasonic tips (EMS: PL4, PL5) that have the shape of a furcation probe. The objective of the small 0.8-mm-diameter sphere on the tip is to increase the surface area at the end of the tip.

Patient acceptance

There are many advantages connected to subgingival ultrasonic instrumentation, both for the operator and the patient. It is generally accepted that most patients prefer the ultrasonic instruments over the hand instruments. They can relax more easily when they are not subjected to sensations of the pushing, pulling, and scraping movements of a curette. Much of the pain felt during subgingival periodontal treatment is caused by instrument pressure on the inflamed gingival tissues. During the maintenance care, when the inflammation of the gingiva has diminished, treatment of subgingival tissues usually is far less invasive than during the initial treatment and examination. Instrumentation with slim ultrasonic tips is often less invasive because these tips fit better into the narrow subgingival space and require less pressure. Recent studies show that patients also prefer ultrasonic instrumentation during the periodontal maintenance care (Croft et al, 2003).

Patient acceptance is an important aspect during periodontal therapy because it affects compliance. With regard to mechanic scalers, the tip movement, type of cooling, size of the tip, and manually versus automatically regulated power settings were studied, but the effect of all these factors on patient comfort or compliance has not been shown convincingly. There are patients who complain about pain during ultrasonic instrumentation even when the greatest caution is observed. In those cases, there is nothing against using hand instruments instead of ultrasonic instruments. Such excessive pain could originate in the periodontal tissues or tooth surface. Experience has demonstrated that some people with hypersensitive root surfaces can experience increased sensitivity following ultrasonic instrumentation. In such cases, hand instruments offer a good solution.

Effectiveness

Professional debridement takes time, both with hand instruments and mechanical scalers. However, there are indications that mechanical scalers increase the effectiveness of the operator (Box 1).

Box 1 Efficiency of ultrasonic instruments:

> Fewer hand instruments are needed.

> Instruments do not have to be sharpened.

> Less time is needed for subgingival debridement.

> Easier removal of "heavy" calculus deposits.

> Local anesthesia is needed less frequently.

> Instruments last longer.

> Better ergonomics, less fatigue for the operator.

The time needed to accomplish a thorough supra- and subgingival debridement is reduced. A recently published meta-analysis shows that the instrumentation time per tooth takes approximately 7.5 minutes with hand instruments and 4.7 minutes with mechanical scalers (Tunkel, 2002). Ultrasonic instrumentation is therefore faster (more effective) than working with hand instruments, but it is still time consuming! Operators who have long-term experience with both instrumentation methods appear to have a preference for ultrasonic debridement. Working with mechanical scalers is less tiring for the operator because only slight pressure on the instrument is needed. This is one of the reasons why fatigue and cramp in the fingers, arm, and shoulder occurs less rapidly. Furthermore, the duration of the learning process seems to be shorter; less clinical experience is needed to become skillful and effective.

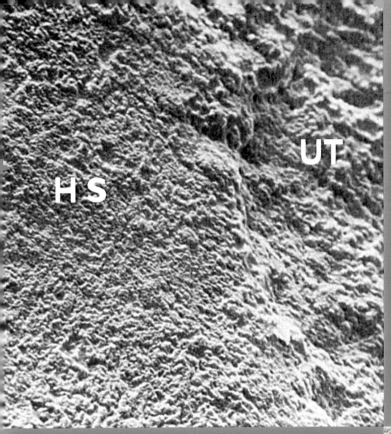

HS UT

Fig 19a SEM photograph (270×) of a root surface that has been instrumented with a Gracey curette. Compare the untouched surface (UT) with the treated surface (HS). It appears that the naturally occurring undulating pattern of the root surface has been removed. This is also called *root planing*. From Pameijer et al, 1972.

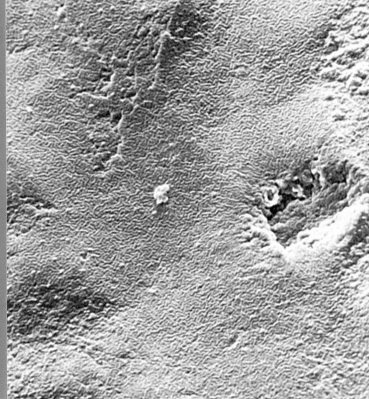

Fig 19b SEM photograph (260×) of a root surface that has been instrumented with an ultrasonic scaler. The undulating pattern of the root surface seems somewhat burnished. From Pameijer et al, 1972.

EFFECTS OF MECHANICAL SCALERS ON THE TOOTH AND SURROUNDING TISSUES

Ultrasonic instruments have the potential to damage both the enamel and radicular surface slightly, as has been shown by light microscopy, profilometry, and scanning electron microscopy. The damage is usually limited and depends on factors such as the amount of pressure placed on the tip, the treatment duration, the shape of the tip, and the power setting of the ultrasonic equipment. Damage to the dental tissues is minimal when the tip is used with slight pressure, an average power setting, and sufficient water cooling.

Research from the 1960s made use of a profilometer to determine the roughness of instrumented surfaces. These assessments provided a "measurement" of the irregularities, but were not capable of determining their "nature." Due to its high resolution, a scanning electron microscope (SEM) is able to show the origin of irregularities, either anatomic or a result of calculus deposits or iatrogenic damage.

Comparative studies between the profilometric assessments and SEM pictures after instrumentation indicate that irregularities often depicted by the profilometer are in fact remains of calculus. Therefore, the picture obtained by the SEM method probably provides more clinically relevant information for the operator.

Effect on the enamel

On intact enamel, ultrasonic instruments cause a reduction in hardness. Clinically, this has little consequence. The area near the cemento-enamel junction is most sensitive to injury. A fine dotted pattern is visible microscopically after instrumentation. On the other hand, the effect on demineralized enamel is disastrous. The decalcified enamel is brushed away by the scaler tip to such an extent that macroscopic cavities are created. As a result, the natural healing of these demineralized surfaces is no longer possible, and the defect will need repair.

Changes of the root surface

The effect of professional debridement with hand instruments or mechanical scalers on the root surface has received a lot of research interest over the years. The results are not unanimous. Several publications report that curettes make the root surface smoother than ultrasonic instruments. SEM has shown that a dentine surface that has been treated with hand instruments shows a regularly striped pattern.

Another study shows that ultrasonic instruments keep the natural, undulating pattern of the root surface intact, and therefore less dental tissue is removed (eg, Pameijer, 1989, see Fig 19). Ultrasonic instruments remove less cementum and expose the dentine only as isolated islands. Comparative studies between sonic and ultrasonic scalers show that the smoothness of the root surface is equal or less when sonic instruments are used. There is limited evidence showing that a smoother root surface is achieved when hand instruments and ultrasonic scalers are used in combination, compared to the use of each of these instruments alone.

The power setting (amplitude) of the ultrasonic unit is probably the variable that has the largest effect on the dental surfaces. Scratches, nicks, and grooves increase exponentially as the power is turned up from average to high (see Fig 13). Surface changes also appear to be directly related to the amount of pressure that is used (Table 3). The risk of damage to the root surface increases the longer the instrument is in contact with the root surface. The total number of instrumentation movements and the instrument angle of the tip also have an effect (see Fig 14). Additionally, the design of the point of the tip and the sharpness of the working surface (a round, blunt tip is preferred) play a role. Given all of these factors, it becomes impossible to reach a unanimous conclusion showing which method of instrumentation, using mechanical scalers, should be advised in order to produce the least possible adverse effect on natural root surfaces.

Nevertheless, the important question remains as to whether it is necessary to obtain a totally smooth root surface to achieve a successful treatment result. It is still unclear to what degree a smooth root surface affects periodontal healing. Moreover, it has never been established that a smooth root surface is synonmous with a totally clean surface.

Table 3 Loss of dental tissue after debridement using various instrumentation forces

Instrument	Force (N)	Root substance loss per 12 strokes (µm)
Ultrasonic scaler	13.8◆	11.6
	27.7	18.2
	55.3	85.9
Sonic scaler	6.9	71.5
	13.8◆	93.5
	27.7	51.1
Curette	34.6	60.2
	69.2◆	108.9
	138.3	264.4
Diamond bur	6.9	94.5
	13.8◆	118.7
	27.7	185.7

◆ Clinically relevant

Based on data from Ritz, Hefti, and Rateitschak, 1991.

Biologically, the roughness of the surface does not seem to play a role in the degree of irritation of the surrounding tissues. In 1956, Waerhaug showed that junctional epithelium adapted well to an irregular root surface. It has even been shown that junctional epithelium can adhere to remaining calculus (Listgarten & Ellegaard, 1973). A rough surface does improve the retention of microbial plaque. Therefore, although there is no hard evidence that a surface has to be totally smooth, instrumentation of the surface until it feels smooth is the best means available to clinically determine that the surface is as clean as possible.

In summary, both instrumentation methods leave irregularities on the root surface. On the basis of current knowledge, it may cautiously be concluded that ultrasonic scalers, used on the average power setting, produce less damage to the root surface than hand instruments or sonic scalers. It appears that instrumentation with an ultrasonic scaler followed by hand instruments leaves the smoothest surface after treatment.

Effect on the pulpal tissue

The thermal and mechanical effects of ultrasonic instruments on the pulp are similar to the use of rotating instruments. There are three factors that can create a temperature rise of the dental tissues:

- Friction between the scaler tip and the tooth surface;
- Direct heat application by the tip and the water coolant;
- Energy absorption of ultrasonic vibrations.

Measurements within the pulp chamber demonstrate that the internal temperature will not increase more than 8°C if the tooth is normally instrumented with water coolant flowing at a rate of 20 ml/min. Without coolant, the temperature in the pulp chamber can rise as much as 35°C. Nerve tissues are particularly susceptible to temperature increases, which can result in an irreversible pulpitis. When ultrasonic energy is absorbed by cells, the cytoplasm and the cell membrane are affected; immature cells are especially sensitive to this phenomenon.

Research has shown that changes may appear in the pulpal tissue at the site of the blood vessels and in the odontoblast layer. The pulp showed an increase in the number of blood vessels and lymphatic vessels and vacuolation of cells. Edema occurred in certain situations. In the odontoblast layer a reduction in the height of these cells was observed and sometimes disorganization and vacuolation took place. Cell necrosis was a rare observation. Some cases showed the irregular formation of tertiary dentine. These changes seem to be in proportion to the time duration of the ultrasonic treatment and, with correct instrument use, appear to be completely reversible. Sufficient cooling, therefore, is essential to minimize possible damage to the pulp tissue.

Effect on periodontal tissues

There are three basic effects on periodontal tissues:
- Thermic (through temperature increase);
- Mechanic (disturbing, tearing of cell membranes);
- Chemical (release of ions).

Little effort has been put into studying the effects of mechanical scalers on periodontal tissues. It seems that ultrasonic instrumentation does not damage surrounding tissues. No negative effects have been reported as a result of energy absorption of ultrasonic vibrations in the periodontal ligament, alveolar bone, and surrounding gingival tissues.

Histologically, ultrasonic instrumentation does show a fragmentation and removal of pocket/sulcus epithelium. Furthermore, a slight expansion of the connective tissue may occur, and local coagulation in the epithelium and connective tissue is possible. These histologic changes are very minor if instrumentation is performed with the intent of removing plaque and calculus from the root surface. The precise way in which the vibrating scaler removes the pocket epithelium is not entirely clear. There are indications of a faster reepithelialization of the pocket after ultrasonic instrumentation in comparison to a treatment with hand instruments. The increased speed of the healing process has been attributed to the spray that develops from the water cooling. This has an additional effect in that bacteria and waste products are flushed away from the surrounding periodontal tissues. Furthermore, the water spray ensures improved visibility of the work field. Currently, no abnormal changes to the alveolar bone, periodontal ligament, or gingival connective tissue are known. Thus, an ultrasonic scaler (for instance with diamond coating at the tip) can also be used safely during flap surgery.

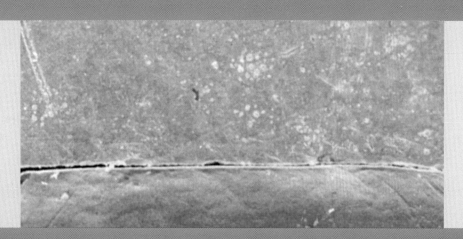

Fig 20a SEM photograph (500×) shows a smooth transition between enamel (bottom) and an amalgam restoration (top) before treatment. From Sivers & Johnson, 1989.

Fig 20b This SEM photograph (500×) shows a rough surface with damage to the edges of the amalgam restoration and the tooth after treatment with a Cavitron scaler. From Sivers & Johnson, 1989.

POSSIBLE SIDE EFFECTS OF MECHANICAL SCALERS

Effect on restorative materials

Restorations in the surrounding area of instrumentation may be damaged (eg, fractures at the margins, scratches, or loss of material). Porcelain restorations are sensitive to fracture. If a composite restoration comes in contact with the ultrasonic tip during its use, a black line frequently appears on the surface, a sign that the tip leaves a trace of metal on the composite surface. This causes the tip to wear unnecessarily. The effect on amalgam surfaces is less evident. A number of studies report changes in the integrity of the restoration surface. The edge of the restoration seems to be particularly sensitive to damage (Fig 20). Other workers find little or no change. In contrast, it appears that mechanical scalers can even be useful for the removal of overhanging amalgam restorations. Normal ultrasonic instrumentation will not have any negative effect on cast metal restorations that have a good fit and are well cemented.

Incidence of a bacteremia

The oral cavity and deepened pockets contain many types of bacteria. The periodontal pocket contains large quantities of microorganisms in the biofilm and in calculus deposits. Moreover, the pocket epithelium is not keratinized. Since the periodontal tissues lie closely in contact with these deposits, they are protected and receive nutrition. During an invasive dental procedure, a break in the epithelial lining of the pocket enables bacteria to enter into the blood circulation. This presence of bacteria in the blood is defined as a *bacteremia*. There is a positive correlation between the severity of the periodontal inflammation and the incidence of bacteremia. The subgingival microflora probably plays an important role in the development of focal infections that originate from the oral environment. A bacteremia can be the cause of a subacute bacterial endocarditis in rheumatic patients and patients with endocardial disorders or cardiovascular prostheses. However, it should be pointed out that bacteremia also has been observed after tooth brushing and the use of interdental toothpicks.

Discussions have arisen concerning the fact that ultrasonic instruments would reduce the chance for bacteremia when compared to hand instrumentation because of:
- Difference in tissue damage;
- Cleaning/rinsing with liquid coolant;
- Possible bactericidal effect of ultrasonic energy in the vicinity of the tip.

Bandt (1964) looked at differences in the occurrence of a bacteremia after instrumentation with hand and ultrasonic instruments. In total, 48 treatments were carried out in which 24 used hand instruments and 24 used ultrasonic instruments. After subgingival instrumentation, approximately 75% of the cases showed a bacteremia irrespective of the instrument used. There was no significant difference between the two instrumentation methods for the number of cases in which a bacteremia was induced. It is remarkable, however, that a relatively high incidence of bacteremia does occur. Patients at risk for endocarditis or other focal infections should therefore always be treated with an antibiotic prophylaxis according to the guidelines of the National Heart Association.

Effect on operators' hands

It has been recognized for a considerable amount of time that vibrations produced by pneumatic hammers may cause the phenomenon of "white fingers" in those operating these machines. The vibrations are transmitted to the hand through direct contact with the hammer, which interrupts the blood circulation of the fingers. The vibration amplitude of these pneumatic tools is large. The vibration amplitude (see Fig 5) of dental mechanical scalers is much smaller. Theoretically, these instruments possess sufficient vibratory power to cause the same phenomenon. Studies so far have not given any indication that the use of mechanical scalers can cause "white fingers" in dental personnel.

Effect on the hearing of the operator/patient

A mechanical scaler is a potential danger to the hearing of both patient and operator. The use of mechanical scalers often involves the production of an intense sound, experienced by some as irritating. It would seem very unlikely that ultrasonic scalers could be potentially harmful, because the vibrations produced lie in a range above auditory perception. The ultrasonic tip itself does not appear to produce any sound, although a slightly perceptible sound can be heard occasionally when the coolant is turned on. The sound heard during treatment appears when the tip comes into contact with a surface and a transformation of the initial "ultrasonic" vibration occurs. The higher the amplitude, the greater the intensity of the sound. Additionally, it has been shown that the sound pitch produced by a piëzo-electric instrument is lower than that of a magnetostrictive instrument. Patients perceive the sound considerably more than the operator. As a result of the vibrations of the ultrasonic instrument being conducted through the air, temporary, reversible effect to the hearing of the operator has been reported. Permanent damage to the hearing has not yet been described, and it seems unlikely that the dental team will incur a hearing loss. Personnel using ultrasonics appear to become accustomed to the noise. It seems that the brain has a "turn off" mechanism after registering the sound for a time. A similar situation occurs when people live in proximity to a railway track: After a certain amount of time they no longer notice the trains passing by.

In the patient, damage could appear by transferal of ultrasonic energy through the teeth and alveolar bone to the inner ear. Tinnitus (ringing in the ears), an early symptom of hearing damage, has been reported after the use of ultrasonic scalers. This seems to occur primarily during the treatment of the molars. The sound is experienced as being uncomfortable by some patients. Not only the level of the tone (frequency) but also the intensity of the sound (decibel) is important when considering damage that can be caused by sound. Up to 85 dB is considered acceptable. On the basis of a number of studies, it is still unclear if the number of decibels produced by an (ultra)sonic tip remains below this limit. A study by Setcos & Mahyuddin (1998) has measured 95 dB as the highest sound level. The study examined short periods of time and focused on the situation when the operator moved the ultrasonic tip around the tooth. They found that during these short time periods, the sound level was mostly below 80 dB.

At present there is no evidence that the patient or dental professional can sustain damage from the peripheral sound of mechanical scalers. Other sources of potentially harmful sound, such as listening to music on a walkman or at a club or pop concert, are far more dangerous, and it is most probable that complaints of patients who are undergoing an ultrasonic treatment are subjective (they just don't like the sound). Those patients who wear hearing aids must be told to turn them off in order to prevent acoustic feedback. If an operator is concerned in any way, or if the peripheral sound produced by (ultra)sonic equipment is experienced as disturbing, then individually made earplugs with a selective filter for high tones can be used. This will remove all sources of concern.

CONTRAINDICATIONS

Shortly after the placement of the first pacemaker (1958), patients with pacemakers were advised to keep away from areas where electromagnetic fields would be able to interfere with their efficacy. In the 1970s the dental office was targeted as a potentially hazardous environment due to various electric units producing electromagnetic fields. Ultrasonic instruments are contraindicated in patients with older types of pacemakers (made before the mid-1980s) and with other electronic "life-support" equipment, as an external electromagnetic field may have a detrimental effect. The newer generation of pacemakers is generally sufficiently protected against electro-magnetic disturbances. They are bipolar and very well isolated. Exceptions for these pacemakers are certain investigatory methods in the medical field (for instance, a scan), electrosurgical instruments, and magneto-strictive ultrasonic scalers (Miller 1998). No interference, as yet, has been established with piëzo-electric ultrasonic scalers. If the operator is in doubt, contact should be sought with the treating cardiologist. The instructions for the use of all currently marketed ultrasonic units state that they should not be used in patients with pacemakers. Sonic scalers are operated by air pressure and do not produce electromagnetic fields. These offer a good alternative for professional debridement risk in patients with pacemakers.

As described earlier, contagious diseases can be transmitted through an aerosol. Walmsley (1988) states that the use of ultrasonic instruments is contraindicated in patients with contagious diseases. The hepatitis virus and HIV have been detected in blood and saliva. In contaminated patients, the risk of cross-contamination by aerosols containing blood and saliva particles is therefore increased. Other authors are less outspoken. They consider the risk of infection with the hepatitis virus via an aerosol unlikely. Transmission of HIV is even less feasible. The danger of contamination via an aerosol is therefore estimated to be rather low to virtually improbable; however, the possibility of potential contamination remains. It has therefore been suggested to use a betadine solution as cooling/irrigation liquid in HIV patients. Whether this contributes in practice to a reduction of the risk is not known. Approximately 4% of the new hepatitis B cases occur in people who, due to their professions, work with human blood. Nonvaccinated members of a dental team have a 2 to 5 times higher risk of becoming infected with hepatitis B in comparison to the population without a professional risk. Therefore vaccination is of great importance.

Tuberculosis is an infection of the airways that can be transmitted by particles released into the air when an infected person coughs in close proximity to another. In Western Europe tuberculosis has almost completely been eliminated. Therefore, for members of a dental team, the risks of becoming infected are low, provided that they meet good protection and infection control standards. Lately however, there have been reports that the number of tuberculosis cases has been increasing. This is particularly so in communities with immigrants, homeless, drug addicts, and HIV patients. Additionally, multi-resistant tuberculosis from Eastern Europe is on the rise. This means that the risk for the dental team will become greater. The production of an aerosol due to instrumentation should be prevented in patients known to be infected with tuberculosis.

These diseases imply that, in principle, each patient is a potential source of contamination. Adequate infection control therefore is important at all times.

In patients with immune systems compromised from disease or medication and in patients with respiratory or swallowing problems, ultrasonic instruments are contraindicated. Furthermore, patients with lung problems are better left untreated with ultrasonic instruments, as the infected aerosol can easily penetrate the lung through aspiration. For these patients, face masks to cover their noses could be used for protection, or the operator can limit the treatment to the use of hand instruments.

A question that often arises is whether pregnant women can work with or be treated with ultrasonic instruments. There is no evidence to indicate that the use of ultrasonic instruments should be avoided during pregnancy. If the patient expresses concern, treatment could be carried out with hand instruments during the period of pregnancy.

Immature growing tissues are sensitive to ultrasonic vibrations. Although there has been no known study, it is generally accepted that ultrasonic instrumentation is contraindicated in children with primary teeth and newly erupted teeth. The immature tissue of the teeth and the buds of permanent teeth can be affected. Because these teeth still have large pulp chambers, there is an increased risk of damage to the pulp tissue. In addition, the enamel of newly erupted permanent teeth is relatively soft, and performing ultrasonic scaling could negatively affect the hardness.

In adult patients, the effect of ultrasonic instrumentation on decalcified enamel is disastrous. The demineralized enamel is brushed away by the scaler tip in such a way that a macroscopic cavity occurs. The natural repair mechanism (remineralization) is no longer possible, and professional restoration of the iatrogenically induced cavity will be necessary. Hypersensitive root surfaces can become even more sensitive (Table 4).

Table 4 Comparing mechanical scalers to hand instruments
After Drisko & Lewis, 1996.

Advantages

Easier, takes less time
Less fatigue for the operator
Fast and easy stain removal
Size of the tip
Shape of the tip
Effective in a static position
Cavitation effect on plaque removal
Better access in furcations
Effective with every movement
Slight pressure
No firm support needed
Less tissue damage
Faster wound healing
Increased tactile sense of pocket topography
Possible bactericidal effect
Irrigation of the pocket
Spray cleans working field
Do not need to be sharpened
Possibility of washing out the pocket with antimicrobial agents
Increased patient comfort and acceptance
Patient preference for ultrasonic instrumentation

Disadvantages

Contaminated aerosol
Expensive
Reduced tactile feeling of root surface
Produces a burnished root surface
Not all handpieces can be sterilized
Aspiration of the spray is needed
Risk of damage to the enamel, dentine
Dentine hypersensitivity, which can temporarily increase
Noisy

Contraindications

Tuberculosis
Compromised immune system
Respiratory problems
Swallowing problems
Primary teeth
Newly erupted teeth
Decalcified enamel
Potential risk for patients with pacemakers
Metal tips with implants

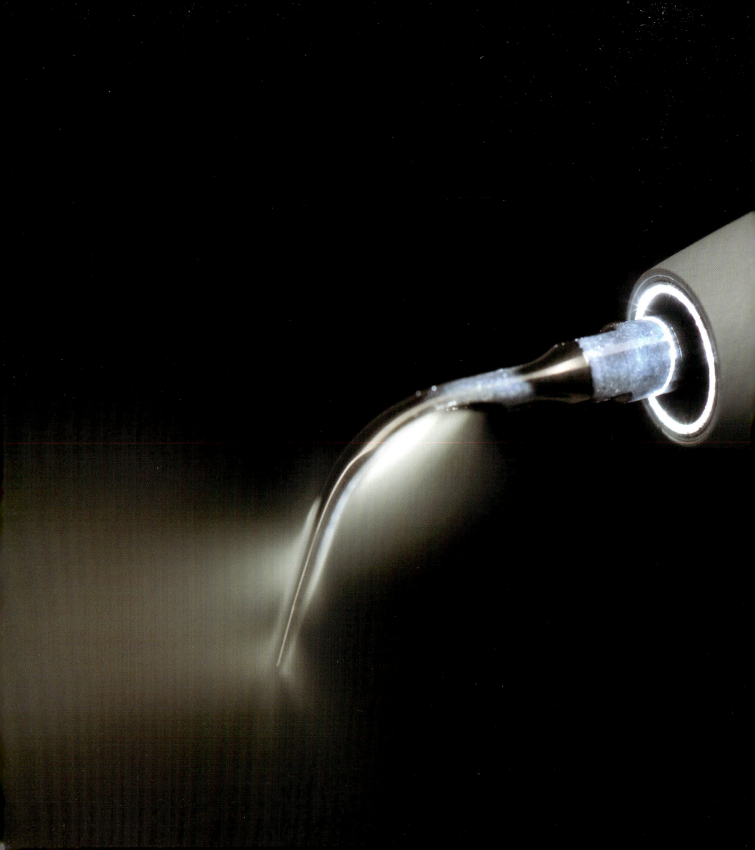

CORRECT APPLICATION OF ULTRASONIC INSTRUMENTS

The use of hand instruments requires, in addition to correct positioning of the scaler or curette, a degree of force that is significant during the active stroke. In contrast, other factors play an important role when mechanical scalers are used. The efficient use of ultrasonic instruments can only be achieved if the operator has adequate knowledge of their mode of action, the correct application, and a structured treatment approach. An effective instrumentation is closely related to a correct technique and one that induces minimal undesirable side effects. As with any new instrument, a new operator should take into account the learning curve.

Although it may appear to be unnecessary repetition of previous topics, it is of utmost importance that before the decision is made to use mechanical scalers, the medical history of the patient be reviewed to ensure that there are no possible contraindications. Explain to the patient, prior to the treatment, what exactly will take place. Demonstrate the ultrasonic scaler and how, due to the water cooling, a spray appears that has to be evacuated. Explain that hearing aids have to be turned off because otherwise they will give acoustic feedback with a high-pitched sound during the treatment.

The tip

The scaler tip must be sterilized prior to each use. During the sterilization process, it is wise to store the scaler tips separately (eg, in a small closed tea strainer) so they cannot be easily lost. Ultrasonic tips are quite expensive; it is easy to discard them when cleaning the surgery after treatment—what a waste that would be! The handpieces also should be handled with care. The crystal elements of the piëzo-electric conductor are not very resistant to shocks (eg, dropping them on the floor).

The movement of the tip is dependent on the design and the frequency. The frequency is dependent on the ultrasonic unit but also determined by the shape of the tip. The power setting determines the deflection of the tip. When the bulk of the tip is orientated longitudinally, it will move in a linear direction. If the bulk is focused more in an eccentric manner, the tip will tend to move laterally. This results in circular, elliptical, or figure-eight movements. The higher the frequency, the less the lateral deflection of the tip. In general, a tip is chosen on the basis of ease and fit for the area to be treated. A tip design must be chosen to reach the apical part of the pocket, since bacterial deposits are present as far apical as the pocket base. A slim tip with a rounded, blunt end makes it possible to clean these areas with minimal tissue damage. The choice of the tip is also dependent on the phase of therapy. Thus, for active periodontal therapy, in which both plaque and calculus deposits have to be removed, a tip will be chosen to provide a relatively high energy transfer (thicker tips at a higher power setting). During maintenance care the therapy focuses primarily on removal of the plaque and biofilm so that slimmer tips can be used at a lower power setting. The surface to be treated determines the required shape of the tip (Table 5).

Table 5 Tip design:

Type	Powersetting	Indication
⟳ EMS: A ⟳ Satelec: 1 of 10p	medium/high	Active phase

• Intended for supragingival debridement.
• Powerful tip for heavy calculus and stain removal.
• Sometimes too powerful for a patient (in such cases use a slimmer tip).

Type	Powersetting	Indication
⟳ EMS: P ⟳ Satelec: 10Z	medium/high	Active phase

• Intended for subgingival debridement.
• Tip with medium power.
• Use up to 3 to 5 mm subgingivally (mostly during initial periodontal treatment).

Type	Powersetting	Indication
⟳ EMS: PS ⟳ Satelec: 1S	low/medium	Active phase Maintenance phase

• Intended for subgingival debridement.
• Low-power tip.
• Tip can be used from 5 mm down to the bottom of the pocket.

Type	Powersetting	Indication
⟳ EMS: PL4, PL5 ⟳ Satelec: TK2-1L, TK2-1R	low/medium	Active phase Maintenance phase

• Intended for subgingival debridement.
• In furcations and root concavities.

Type	Powersetting	Indication
⊃ EMS: PL1, PL2 ⊃ Satelec: TK2-1L, TK2-1R	low/medium	Maintenance phase

- A curved version of the PL3/TK1-1S.
- Intended for subgingival debridement.
- Tip with minimal power (as PL3 tip).
- In furcations and distal of the last molar.
- Can be used as an alternative for the PL4/PL5.

Type	Powersetting	Indication
⊃ EMS: PL3 ⊃ Satelec: TK1-1S, TK1-1L	low/medium	Maintenance phase

- Intended for subgingival debridement.
- Tip with minimal power.

Type	Powersetting	Indication
⊃ EMS: HPL3, DPL3 ⊃ Satelec: H1, H2L, H2R	low/medium	Surgery

- Slim tip with diamond coating.
- Intended to use with direct vision.

Type	Powersetting	Indication
⊃ EMS: PI-implant ⊃ Satelec: PH2L, PH1, PH2R	low/medium	Maintenance phase Implant maintenance

- Plastic tip (EMS) or carbon fiber (Satelec).
- Intended for supra- and subgingival debridement.
- Safe to use on titanium surfaces.

There are many tips of varying shape and size for (ultra)sonic mechanical scalers. The tips are designed in such a way that the area to be cleaned can be optimally reached with specific tips for supra- and subgingival areas. For supragingival use, the tips are usually thicker and adjusted to the shape of the tooth surface. Short, thicker tips are powerful, and their shape is suited to removing the heavier calculus deposits. The size of the tip makes it possible to clean a large area; these tips are suited to the removal of large quantities of calculus. The tips for subgingival use are straight with a blunt end. Some of these are shaped like a curette. There is, however, no need for sharp instruments since the movement of the tip loosens the calculus through vibrations. This explains why tips with a rounded, blunt end, when used with horizontal, vertical, and angulated movements, are sufficiently effective. Currently, there are specifically designed long, thin straight perio-tips for extra-deep subgingival debridement (Fig 21). These new tips are easier to use than curettes and can penetrate more apically, and the treatment is faster. An additional benefit is that they do not have to be sharpened. The slim, elegant tip shape makes it possible to explore the pocket before, during, and after the active use. The treatment results are usually evaluated with a periodontal pocket probe but during the process of treatment can even be carried out with an inactive ultrasonic tip.

It should be taken into account when using thin tips that the longer and thinner the tip is, the less power that is transferred to the tooth surface. Furthermore, the thinner shaft also reduces the power. The operator will therefore have to spend more time in removing the subgingival calculus. Some ultrasonic systems provide long, very thin tips that are intended for periodontal maintenance care. These tips have limited power, and little energy is transferred to the surface. They are very suitable for plaque removal and are relatively safe for the root surface and therefore can be applied during regular maintenance care.

For the cleaning of furcations and concavities on the root surface, curved tips are available. These resemble a furcation probe and can be introduced into the furcation with a rotational movement (see Fig 21a). The PL4 and PL5 from EMS have a small 0.8-mm-diameter sphere at the end of the tip. The sphere increases the working surface area when compared to straight-ended tips. These furcation tips are manufactured in both a left and right design. An added advantage is provided by tips with a diamond coating (70 µm) applied to the tip shaft. However, care should be taken, since diamond-coated tips remove five times as much tooth structure as regular, uncoated metal tips. Diamond tips should only be used with direct vision, otherwise

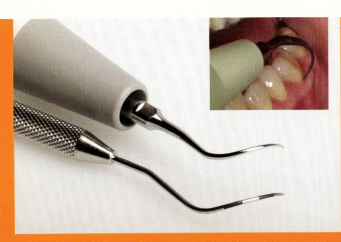

Fig 21a Ultrasonic tips that have the shape of a furcation probe make the furcation area more accessible.

Fig 21b Slim, elegant scaler tips make efficient, professional supra- and subgingival debridement possible.

it is possible to reduce the volume of dental tissues excessively. During periodontal surgery, diamond-coated tips appear to be especially useful and enhance the operator's ability to remove calculus and smooth root surfaces. Instrumentation can be carried out effectively in the complex anatomy of alveolar bone and root surface.

In practice, the effectiveness of the ultrasonic tip is reduced if the operator places too much pressure on the root surface. The ultrasonic vibrations and amplitude no longer function optimally. Depending on the manufacturer, newer piëzo-electric units have feedback systems that check the frequency and amplitude 40 times per second and automatically adjust these parameters. They function in a way similar to a "cruise control" within the ultrasonic handpiece.

Ultrasonic tips do not last forever but wear down and even break when they become thinner. As a result, the point of resonance no longer corresponds with the end of the tip. The consequences of this are unclear, but probably the vibrations will decrease. A worn tip reduces the efficiency, and more time or a higher power setting is required to obtain adequate debridement. When the tip has lost 1 mm of its length, the reduction in efficiency is about 25%; with 2 mm, it is approximately 50%. This applies in all probability to the slimmer tips. Various manufacturers provide simple cards that allow the tip to be checked to determine whether or not a tip needs replacing (Fig 22). The choice appears rather arbitrary when

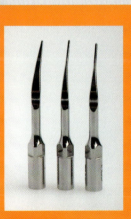

Fig 21c
Alternate view of scaler tips. (EMS: P, PS, PL3).

Fig 22
Tip cards on which the manufacturers have indicated when a tip needs to be replaced.

questioning the manufacturer; the operator should use clinical experience to decide at what point the tip should be discarded. A worn-down tip will become more pointed, but it can be rounded using a rubber wheel to make the metal smooth and shiny again. The longer and thinner tips are more fragile, and there is a possibility of damage and breakage during use or the sterilization process. Bending back a distorted tip is not possible and results in uncontrolled tip movements. Additionally, distortion encourages metal fatigue and increases the chance of breakage.

Although a great variety of tips is available, an adequate ultrasonic kit consists of a few (two to four) types. The number of different tips that are needed for successful treatment is less than the number of hand instruments required. Since the tips do not have to be sharpened, they will last a long time if treated correctly. The operator will need approximately three to four tips of each type for an average working day, when it is possible to sterilize them between patients.

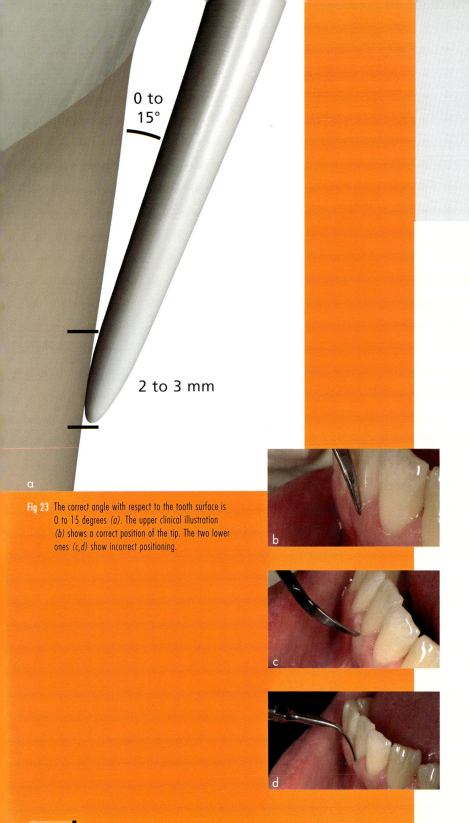

0 to 15°

2 to 3 mm

a

Fig 23 The correct angle with respect to the tooth surface is 0 to 15 degrees *(a)*. The upper clinical illustration *(b)* shows a correct position of the tip. The two lower ones *(c,d)* show incorrect positioning.

b

c

d

Differences in ultrasonic units result in different vibratory movements of the scaler tips. As described previously, the tips can make linear, elliptic, circular, or figure-eight movements. The ultrasonic tip must be placed in such a way that the pattern of the vibrations is optimally oriented with respect to the tooth surface, and the tip itself has to be placed at the correct angle with respect to the tooth surface. It should not be placed with the point against the surface (Fig 23), otherwise the scaler tip will tap against the tooth, which is painful for the patient. Additionally, this could damage the surface. For example, a tip which vibrates principally backward and forward (linear movement) should be placed parallel to the tooth surface. A simple exercise to see if placement is correct is to hold the tip against a small glass plate or the torque-control key. The sound should be even and low. If the position is not correct, a high-pitched sound will be audible and scratches will appear on the surface.

Adjustment of ultrasonic units

Most ultrasonic units have two control buttons with which to regulate the power and the liquid coolant. These must be adjusted correctly prior to the treatment. Depending on the type of the equipment that is chosen, the frequency either can be adjusted manually or regulated automatically by the unit. With a correct setting of the power and cooling, a maximum efficiency of the instrument will be obtained. This reduces the fatigue of the operator and makes the treatment more pleasant for the patient.

Power adjustment

The power button regulates the energy supply and thus affects the deflection (amplitude) of the tip. The power setting is different for each brand and should be individually adjusted to the *minimum effective power*. The operator will, with time, gain sufficient experience to develop a "feel" for the optimal setting. In addition to the power setting, there are a number of other factors that affect the energy transferal to the tooth surface:

- Instrumentation time: The longer a surface is treated the greater the amount of energy.
- Applied pressure: The amount of pressure influences the effectiveness of the active part of the tip. If there is too much pressure, the effectiveness will be reduced or the end of the tip may even stop vibrating.
- Shape of the tip: Sharper tips will be more effective. However, to minimize the risk of damage to the hard and soft tissues, a blunt and rounded tip is preferred.
- Angle of the tip with respect to the surface: The greater the angle, the more energy transfer takes place. As a guideline, the tip should be positioned at an angle of 15 degrees or less with respect to the tooth surface.

Studies have shown that during initial periodontal treatment, a medium power setting produces similar clinical results as working at maximum power. When the power is turned up, the possibility of damage to the tissue of the tooth increases. With a setting that is too high, the number of vibrations increase to such an extent that the tip will produce a hammering effect. There are two methods for setting the power at the correct level. First, there is the arbitrary setting in which the power is set as indicated by the manufacturer in the operator's manual.

The second and preferred method compensates for the variations that have been observed during the use of the individual scaler tips. One should therefore start at a low power setting and slowly increase it until the tip functions optimally. This ensures that the minimum effective setting is obtained. The power of a sonic scaler is adjusted by the manufacturer and is dependent on the air pressure of the dental unit.

Adjustment of liquid coolant

Previously in this text, it was demonstrated that the ultimate effect of the mechanical scaler primarily takes place through the vibrations of the tip. The vibrations generate heat, which can be harmful to the surrounding tissues; therefore, it is essential to provide a coolant. The water supply providing the coolant runs through a tube from the unit to the handpiece and the tip. There are tips with either internal or external cooling. The most important objective is to cool the end of the tip adequately.

At the start of the working day and prior to the first patient, the unit has to be flushed a full 2 minutes to remove any residual contaminated water left in the tubing. Contamination of the tubing can be counteracted by choosing a unit with its own water reservoir in which an antimicrobial or sterile water/saline can be added.

It is necessary to check and possibly adjust the water pressure for each tip being used. In general, the water pressure is adjusted correctly when it appears automatically on the tip as a fine spray. Adjustment of the water spray frequency will also affect the quality of the spray. Generally, the tip has the correct frequency of vibrations when a fine spray is formed at the end of the tip, possibly with the forming of a drop at the point. If too much water flows to the tip, the stream of water will be so excessive that the operator will have to concentrate more on aspiration than the actual work of removing plaque and deposits.

The use of a mouth mirror simultaneously with instruments that have a flow of water coolant is impractical since the mirror will continuously be coated with water. This problem can be partially solved if the operator wipes a gloved finger over the mirror surface. This has the effect of allowing the water droplets to coalesce into a single layer of water. Some operators also find it hard to detect calculus on the tooth surface in a moist environment. It may therefore be necessary to use an air syringe to dry the surface of the tooth to check for remnants of calculus deposits.

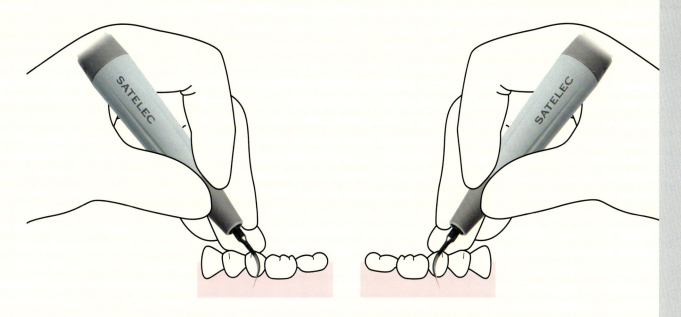

Fig 24 Modified pen grip for the left and right hand. An instrument is held with the thumb, index finger, and middle finger. The ring finger is used for support. Modified after Wilkins, 1999.

Technique

Most tips can be used when the operator sits in the 12 o'clock position. The handpiece can be held with either the pen grip or the modified pen grip, depending on the preference of the operator (Fig 24). A light grip is important in order to exercise light pressure. The handpiece should be held loosely between thumb and fingers. Basically, the handpiece is held at the point of transition from handpiece to the tip. Sometimes access to parts of the dentition is limited, so it becomes necessary to hold the handpiece further toward its base.

The pressure that is exercised on the handpiece is comparable to the forces that are used during periodontal probing. Of course sufficient force has to be used to make sure that the tip actually makes contact with the tooth surface. The minimum effective pressure an operator can exercise is approximately 0.5 N. Light pressure increases the tactile feeling. It also prevents the vibrations of the tip from being suppressed by the lateral forces and reduces damage to the tissue. The movement of the tip must be carried out with care but also with definitive strokes.

The thicker standard tips have a relatively powerful vibration. In order to support the tip movement, it can be of help to place the ring finger intraorally to provide a support position close to the working field. With the slimmer tips, support further from the working field will also suffice, using, for example, the contralateral side of the dental arch or extraorally on the chin or cheek. In comparison to hand instruments, this support requires little pressure, which is clearly noticeable to the operator at the end of the day, since it is much less tiring. The positioning of the supporting fingers will also determine where the handpiece is to be held. When the position is further from the working field, it will automatically be necessary to hold the handpiece further toward its base. When searching for a firm support position, the operator can actually produce a negative effect because of the similarity of working with hand instruments; the operator could be encouraged to use too much force. Once again, this is not desirable for effective use of a mechanical scaler.

Fig. 25 Start with horizontal sweeping movements with the working end of the tip (approximately 2 to 3 mm) in contact with the tooth. This is followed by moving the instrument both apically and coronally.

(Left) Due to the relatively small contact surface at the end of the scaler tip, the debridement must be performed systematically, covering small areas.

(Right) In comparison, the active stroke of a hand instrument leads to the removal of a rectangular area of the debris within the working field.

Modified after Petersilka & Flemmig, 1999.

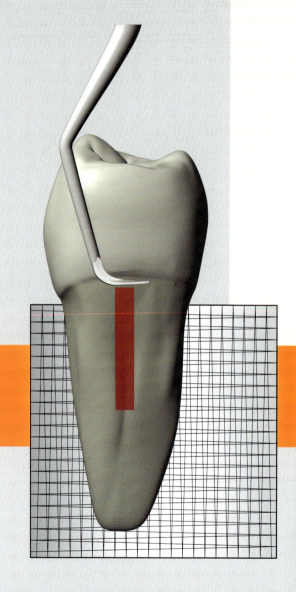

As described previously, the side of the tip of most ultrasonic systems should be held against the tooth tangentially. The natural, rounded shape of the tooth should be taken into account. The last 2 to 3 mm of the tip must be in contact with the enamel or root surface that needs to be cleaned. Holding the tip perpendicularly to the tooth damages the surface and therefore should be avoided. Using the side of the tip, the operator systematically cleans the tooth surface over a small area. Therefore, it is recommended to mentally divide the subgingival root surface into a number of small squares. For each area, the surface is treated with vertical and overlapping movements of the tip starting at the base. This is then repeated in the horizontal direction (Fig 25). The objective of the vertical and horizontal movements is to contact as great a surface area as possible. A good way of visualizing the importance and effect of these movements is to draw the same overlapping lines in pen on a small square of paper until it is completely covered by ink (see Fig 25). It readily becomes apparent that it is very difficult to fill in the area sufficiently with only vertical lines. Therefore, additional horizontal lines are needed. Another good exercise is to try to remove the dried, brown deposits of coffee from a mug without damaging the glazing.

It is advisable to keep the tip in motion during instrumentation in order to avoid an unnecessary temperature increase on the treated surface. With light pressure the tip should be moved back and forth, always maintaining contact with the enamel or root surface. Light pressure is not always easy to maintain. The vibrations of the tip produce a reduced tactile feeling between the tip and the tooth surface. The operator may be inclined to exercise too much pressure on the tip because of this reduced tactile perception, especially when working in narrow, deep pockets. This may produce a rough root surface.

In the subgingival area the tip must remain in contact with the root surface as much as possible to prevent unnecessary damage to the gingival tissues. During instrumentation, it is advisable to avoid rapid or rough movements. Instrumentation should not be hurried despite the fact that the apparatus stimulates the idea that one must work with speed. Rushed treatment is inefficient and may cause unnecessary damage to the hard and soft oral tissues.

A slow, accurate instrumentation technique can prevent damage to the attachment, particularly in narrow pockets or in situations where the attachment level (the base of the pocket) has an irregular form. When the instrumentation is complete the gingiva should not look ragged, with loose tissue fragments or split papillae. Once the operator has learned to manage these basic principles, the time is ripe for more creative applications to be undertaken.

The thorough cleaning of furcations is very difficult. Even when using ultrasonic instruments it is rarely possible to clean the root surface 100%. Researchers who have intensively studied this difficulty suggest that odontoplasty, possibly with a diamond-coated tips, should be performed to improve access to furcations with a limited opening. Widening of the furcation entrance will increase the chance of success.

Fig 26 Hygoformic aspirators.

It has been established that a full-time dental hygienist applies approximately 32 tons of scaling force per year and makes approximately 25,000 scaling movements. The cumulative effect of all this may cause operator injury to the joints of the thumb, wrist, and shoulder (Wilkins, 1999). Mechanical scalers have a clear advantage in this respect compared with hand instruments, since working with them is less tiring. A disadvantage is the need to aspirate the water coolant. However, the coolant cleanses the working field, providing a better view, and therefore reduces the need to constantly reach for the multi-functional syringe. For those working without an assistant, the instrumentation technique requires some practice. One hand holds the aspirator while the other hand holds the ultrasonic handpiece. The aspirator tip can also be used to retract the cheek, tongue, and lips. A cup-shaped area is formed in which fluid collects and is therefore easy to evacuate. This will enable the operator to control the amount of water in the mouth and also to reduce the amount of aerosol.

Using a mirror for indirect vision or reflecting light onto the working field is generally difficult, since it requires an extra hand and also because the mirror surface becomes misted. If a mirror is required, then a low-volume aspirator can be placed to one side of the mouth. The operator will have one hand free for the mirror, avoiding overflow of water from the patient's mouth. For example, the circular coiled aspirator, Hygoformic (Fig 26), can be used for this purpose. The aspirator tube is then brought from the back of the chair into the mouth.

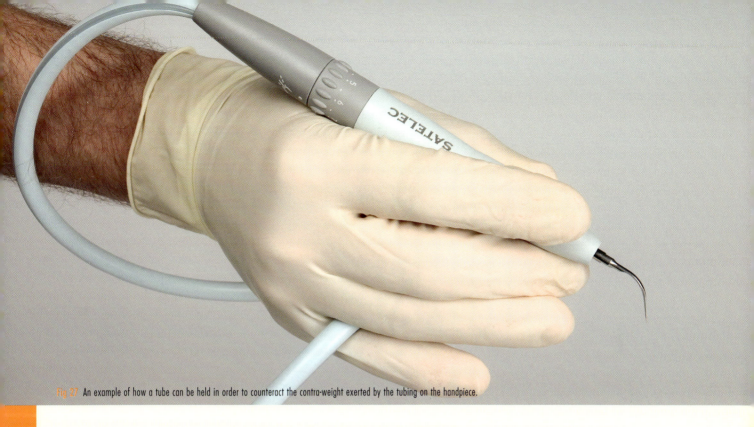

Fig 27 An example of how a tube can be held in order to counteract the contra-weight exerted by the tubing on the handpiece.

Twisting of the tubing that connects the handpiece with the unit must be avoided, since this would cause too much muscular tension in the arm of the operator. In order to reduce the weight of the tubing, it can be placed across the shoulder of the operator, across the handle of the surgical lamp, or held in a loop between the ring finger and the little finger (Fig 27). By reducing the weight on the hands of the operator, the tactile perception will increase. When adapting the tip to the rounded contours of a tooth surface, the operator will have to rotate the handpiece between the fingers. The tubing will, however, offer a degree of resistance and will tend to twist back to its original position. When trying out different brands of ultrasonic units, the operator will notice that the stiffness of the tubing differs with different models; one brand will offer more resistance than another.

Fig 28 Periodontal treatment protocol.

DIAGNOSIS

TREATMENT PLAN   Active phase

PROFESSIONAL
DEBRIDEMENT

POSSIBLE SURGERY   Surgical phase

MAINTENANCE CARE   Recall phase

SYSTEMATIC TREATMENT WITH MECHANICAL SCALERS

It should now be apparent that a systematic choice should be made when deciding on which tip to use in a mechanical scaler, and in this respect it is essential to have a clear overview of the different treatment phases: the active phase in gingivitis patients, the active phase of professional debridement in periodontal patients, and professional prophylaxis during periodontal maintenance care (Fig 28).

In addition to a correct systematic approach to treatment and instrumentation method, the operator must also be adequately trained in pocket topography and root anatomy in order to clean a pocket adequately. Prior to the start of the treatment, it is essential to make an accurate periodontal chart on which probing depths and furcation anatomy have been recorded. Moreover, a sufficient number of radiographs should be available—preferably a full set of intraoral films. This information provides the operator with a mental picture of the pocket anatomy. (Ultra)sonic instruments are used as a part of the total treatment approach in a well-constructed treatment plan.

For a periodontal patient

For an efficient, professional supra- and subgingival debridement in a periodontal patient, it is wise to divide the mouth into four quadrants. It is both unnecessary and contraindicated to clean the entire dentition superficially first and work more thoroughly later. A pocket must be cleaned from its most apical part coronally. If plaque and/or calculus remain in the apical part of the pocket while the marginal part of the periodontium heals, this could result in blockage of the flow of inflammatory exudates out of the pocket. This increases the risk of forming a periodontal abscess. Furthermore, a pocket with a tight, healthy gingival collar presents resistance to entry with an instrument.

For the comfort of the patient, it is recommended to clean the deep and inflamed pockets under local anesthesia during the active phase of periodontal treatment. By working by quadrant, the supra- and subgingival debridement for each specific area can be performed optimally in one session under more relaxed working conditions with the use of local anesthesia. The recommended systematic approach is illustrated in figures 29 and 30.

For example, start the treatment in the first quadrant on the buccal side from the distal surface of the last molar, moving in the direction of the free surface on the buccal side of this molar. Adjust the angle of the handpiece with respect to the tooth surface in such a way that the tip is always applied using its lateral surface. Continue toward the mesial surface. Then proceed to the neighboring tooth from the distal surface via the free surface towards the mesial side and so on for each tooth to the midline. Subsequently, the same systematic approach can be applied on the palatal side. A choice can be made to start working from the midline posteriorly or to proceed in the same way as on the buccal side from the distal surface of the last molar. In order to reach the palatal surfaces, the patient's head should be turned a little (eg, to the right for right-handed operators in the 12 o'clock position) so that the lateral surface of the ultrasonic tip contacts the dental tissues. In this way, the operator sits in the best possible position to use the tips correctly. A tip may occasionally become locked in between two teeth, causing the vibrations to almost completely disappear. Under these circumstances, carefully loosen the tip and try again.

Maintenance care/gingivitis treatment

In periodontal maintenance care or in gingivitis treatment, debridement of the entire dentition in one single session is feasible. Following a specific systematic approach is recommended. A good option is as follows (see Fig 29): Start the treatment in the

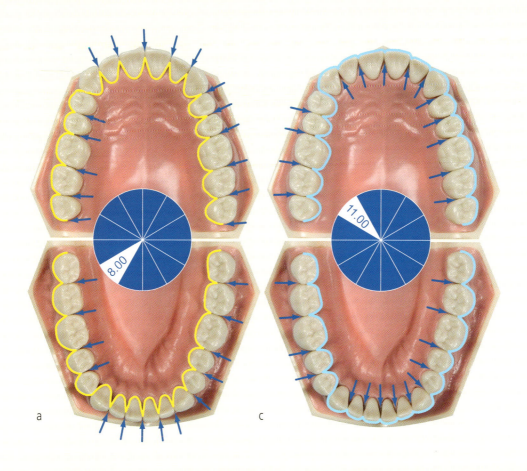

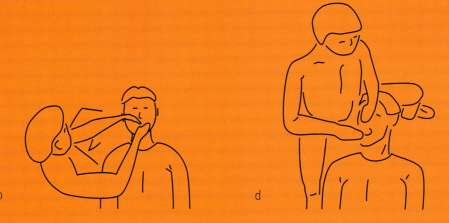

Fig 29 Systematic treatment for professional debridement of the entire dentition in a single session. *(Left, a and b)* The *yellow line* indicates the first round for both maxillary and mandibular dentitions; the operator's position is at 8 o'clock. *(Right, c and d)* In *blue*, the route taken back is shown; the operator's position is at 11 o'clock. The interproximal areas are often harder to reach, so the scaler tip may be used with an angulated approach (see also Fig 30b) or possibly even horizontaly, as shown by the dark *blue arrows*. Modified after Petersilka & Flemmig, 1999.

first quadrant on the buccal side from the distal surface of the last molar. Work across the free surface on the buccal side toward the mesial side of this molar. Ensure that the tip is applied using its lateral surface as much as possible. Then proceed to the neighboring tooth from the distal surface via the free surface toward the mesial side and continue to the midline. Then, with the patient's head in the same position, continue to the second quadrant palatally and interproximally through to the distal side of the last maxillary molar on the left side. An alternative would be to proceed from the distopalatal side of the last molar in the second quadrant, to the left central incisor. The head of the patient is then turned, and treatment continues on the buccal side of the second quadrant, starting from the distal surface of the last molar mesially to the left central incisor and via the palatal surface of the right central incisor toward the distal side of the last molar in the first quadrant. For the mandible, the same systematic approach can be applied. By keeping to a consistent systematic approach, no areas of the dentition will be overlooked, ensuring that all surfaces of the dentition are cleaned thoroughly.

Instrumentation

During instrumentation, the point of the tip is almost always directed apically (see Fig 30a). This is a relatively simple procedure on the buccal and lingual surfaces, but it may present problems in the less easily accessible interproximal sites. The tip should be rotated in a slightly angulated position to approach the interproximal area (see Fig 30b). The tip should be held in contact with the tooth surface as much as possible to prevent the patient from experiencing a "shuddering" effect every time renewed contact with the tooth is established. Overlapping, sweeping horizontal movements are made back and forth holding the tip at an angle of 15 degrees (or less) in relation to the tooth surface. The first 2 to 3 mm of the instrument, as measured from the point of the tip, should be kept in contact with the surface. This back and forth movement can be alternated with overlapping, vertical movements, in a similar fashion to pocket probing (see Fig 25). Interproximal surfaces can be cleaned using, as a compromise, an angulated direction of the tip. By approaching the deposits on the tooth surface from different directions, plaque and calculus will be more readily loosened and removed. The tip must be kept continuously in motion, but the sweeping movements to remove the plaque and calculus should be performed slowly and with care. In order to smooth the surface of a tooth following removal of plaque and calculus, it may help to make faster, lighter movements across the surface (also called the *vibrato* movement). The point must never be placed perpendicular to the tooth, because this will cause iatrogenic damage to the dental tissues. Instrumentation of furcations is best achieved with the slimmer, curved tips. The two or three roots are treated as separate teeth using the protocol already described. By using these tips and tricks, which are summarized in Box 2, a satisfactory clinical result can be obtained (Fig 31).

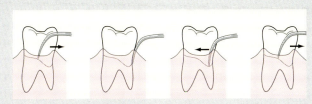

Fig 30a The tip is first moved horizontally with overlapping back-and-forth "sweeping" movements, working from the base of the pocket coronally (vestibular view). Modified after Darby & Walsh, 2003.

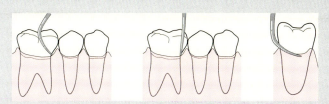

Fig 30b The interproximal approach is often more difficult. In such a case the tip can be entered in a slightly angulated position, preferably with the tip pointing in the direction of the apex. Modified after Darby & Walsh, 2003.

Box 2 Guidelines for the use of ultrasonic instruments:

> Check the medical history for contraindications.
> Ask the patient to turn off hearing aids.
> Construct a systematic plan of approach, based on the pocket/periodontium chart.
> Have the patient rinse for 1 minute with chlorhexidine before the treatment.
> Use sufficient water cooling to prevent overheating of the instrument and tooth surfaces.
> Use the water button to adjust the correct amount of cooling. The end of the tip must produce a mist without issuing a stream of water.
> Power setting on average or low.
> Hold the handle in the pen grip or in the modified pen grip.
> Place the tip against the tooth surface at an angle of approximately 15 degrees.
> Hold the tip parallel to the longitudinal axis of the tooth as much as possible.
> Place the side of the instrument against the tooth surface (not the point).
> Use primarily the side of the tip with the point apically directed.
> Never use the point.
> Use a continuous, overlapping, back-and-forth, sweeping movement.
> Use little force.
> With the thin (slim) tips, the sweeping movement is slower than with the thicker types.
> Rotate the handpiece between the fingers in order to obtain the correct position for working in different locations in the mouth.
> Use a face mask and protective glasses during the treatment.
> Use a high-volume aspirator to minimize the aerosol.
> Do not hold the aspirator too close to the tip of the scaler or else the cooling will be insufficient.
> Check the tooth surface after treatment with a periodontal probe or with the ultrasonic tip when it is not in operation.
> Do not use ultrasonic instruments in patients with pacemakers without consulting their physician/cardiologist first.
> Prior to use, allow the coolant to run for 2 minutes to minimize the bacterial contamination of the tubing and the water reservoir.
> Ultrasonic instruments should not be used with porcelain restorations.
> Only use an ultrasonic scaler briefly on cemented restorations.

Fig 31 Clinical results with an ultrasonic scaler.

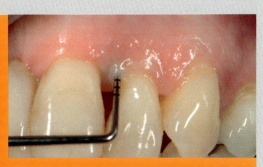

Fig 31a Pocket of 8 mm mesial of the left lateral incisor.

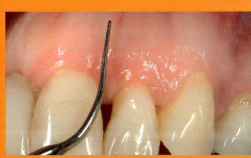

Fig 31b The tip length indicates the depth to be reached during cleaning.

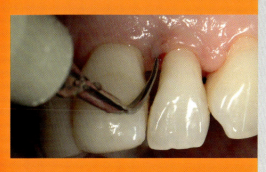

Fig 31c After the administration of the local anesthesia, the tip is placed in the pocket, and the root surface is thoroughly cleaned.

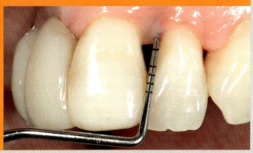

Fig 31d Four months after ultrasonic instrumentation and thorough oral hygiene instructions, a pocket reduction of 4 mm has taken place.

Fig 32 The new generation of handpieces with an illuminated tip (P-max lux, Satelec).

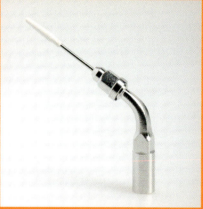

Fig 33a Designed for implants, the straight plastic tip of EMS (PI-implant) has to be placed in the endo-chuck.

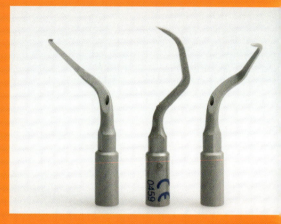

Fig 33b The carbon fiber tips of Satelec are available in curette-like models (PH2L, PH1, PH2R).

NEW DEVELOPMENTS

Currently there are piëzo-electric units with handpieces providing illumination of the tip for better vision (Fig 32). Some authors also advise working with magnification that enlarges 2 to 3 times for even better vision. A recent development, which is still in its infancy, is a fiber optic light attached to the mechanical scaler to illuminate the tooth surface. The root surface is cleaned thoroughly with the mechanical scaler, once the papillae is slighty reflected to facilitate instrumentation. Two studies have reported promising results. Treatment using the sonic scaler with fiber optics and reflection of the papilla was compared with a normal closed instrumentation without illumination. The new instrumentation method produced a significantly better cleaning. After the treatment with closed scaling, 5% of the calculus remained, while following scaling with fiber optics, only 2% of the calculus could be found. In comparison, the control surfaces had, on average, 39% coverage with calculus deposits.

Another development is the introduction of plastic and carbon fiber tips (Fig 33). An invitro SEM study showed that plastic tips removed less dental tissue and left an even smoother surface behind than a metal tip, even smoother than that found after the use of a curette and polishing with a rubber cup and polishing paste. These tips are therefore indicated during periodontal maintenance care as well as for the cleaning of implants (Gagnot et al, 1999).

At present, one manufacturer is working on a piëzo-electric unit and tips that allow the operator to prepare bone. This would be of great use in the field of implant dentistry in cases requiring a sinus floor elevation. The ultrasonic tip would be able to work its way through the hard bony tissue, but less easily through the soft tissue, thus preventing a perforation of the membrane of the sinus floor. This development still has to be evaluated in practice.

Fig 34 Vector ultrasonic unit from Durr.

Figure 34 shows the Vector systems from the manufachurer Durr, an unusual addition to the piëzo-electric market. The instrument, however, is not a mechanical scaler but is designed to transfer ultrasonic vibrations to the subgingival area. By combining this vibration with an abrasive or polishing paste, the tooth surface is cleaned without direct contact between the tip and the tooth surface (or so the manufacturer claims). It is assumed that the micro-streaming and cavitation forces are adequate to achieve this objective. There is still insufficient research to support this assumption (Sculean et al, 2004). However, the manufacturer has recently introduced a new handpiece. This is a mechanical scaler and works in a comparable fashion to the EMS and Satelec.

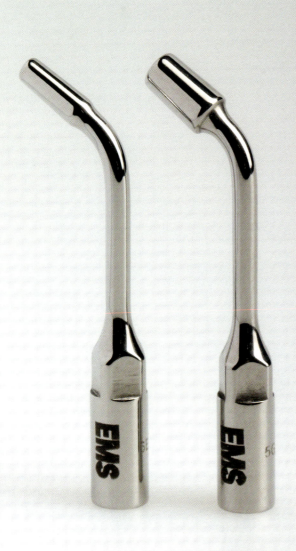

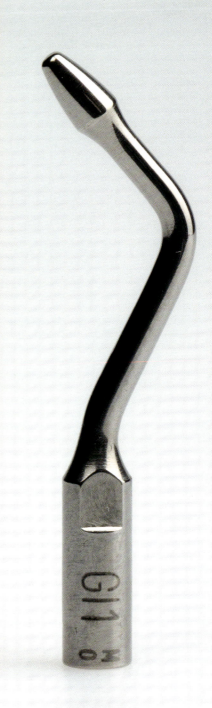

Fig 35 Tips of EMS (F, E) and Satelec (GI1) to enhance the setting of glass-ionomer cements.

DENTAL APPLICATIONS OUTSIDE PERIODONTAL THERAPY

Enhanced setting of glass-ionomer cement

Glass-ionomer cements adhere well to the tooth structure but are too weak and sensitive to wear in the early stage of hardening; the full strength for these materials is only reached after a few weeks. Light curing of glass-ionomer and compomers solve a small portion of these problems but at the same time introduce new problems, such as a lower resistance to wear. The latest generation of glass-ionomer cements with a high fill have a better compressive and flexible strength and a higher resistance to wear. The resistance to wear of a completely hardened glass-ionomer is at least as good as that of composite filling material. With the help of ultrasonic instruments, it is possible to reduce the setting time by 90% and to improve a number of the material's characteristics. This increases the range of use of conventional glass-ionomer to the premolar and molar areas in the permanent dentition. The application of ultrasound generated by a dental ultrasonic instrument enables glass-ionomer to harden within 20 to 40 seconds. The idea was initiated by Van Asperen from the Netherlands. At the Academic Centre for Dentistry in Amsterdam (ACTA), work on this phenomenon is continuing with the aid of EMS and Satelec. The work currently being carried out is directed at making the technique more user friendly by developing special tips, examples of which can be seen in Fig 35. Ultimately, the objective is to produce a rapid and ready-to-use product, which will allow large, reliable restorations to be placed in the posterior dentition. Recent developments within this field of research have shown that any form of energy supplied during the setting process will result in an improved glass-ionomer restoration. A light-curing lamp with a high capacity has the same effect.

Ultrasound in endodontics

The dental application of ultrasonics was limited mainly to periodontics, until Richman, in 1957, introduced this technique into endodontics. However, it took almost 20 years before a commercial system to prepare and clean root canals ultrasonically was developed (ie, Endosonics) by Howard Martin. The first devices were simply a modification of the existing equipment: eg, Dentsply's Cavi-Endo was based on its Cavitron. For a variety of commercial and practical reasons, Endosonics was forgotten. For example, the instruments were sensitive to vibrations, and during ultrasonic preparation of root canals, the cutting motion of the files was uncontrolled, which sometimes led to damage in the apical part of the canal and/or an irregular canal wall. Recently, there has been a renewed interest in the application of ultrasonics in endodontics. Due to the development of special equipment, the applications in which it can be used are now much broader than before.

Ultrasonics within endodontics is now used for:
- Irrigation of root canals;
- Periapical surgery;
- Removal of posts, broken instruments, and other obstacles from the root canal;
- Condensing of gutta-percha;

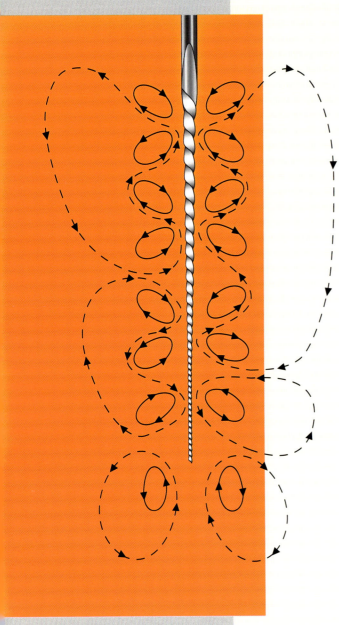

Fig 36 Theoretic pattern of micro-streaming around an
ultrasonic irrigation tip. Modified after Ahmad
et al, 1987.

- Access to the root canal;
- Distribution of cement in the root canal.

Irrigation of root canals

Cleaning and shaping of the root canal systems are important steps during a root canal treatment. The objectives of root canal treatment are not only to remove pulp tissue, dentine debris, and microorganisms, but also to shape the root canal in such a way that it can be filled from the canal entrance to the apical foramen. Due to the complex anatomy of the root canal system, however, it is impossible to clean the system completely with just files and reamers. Even with new, advanced instruments constructed of nickel-titanium (NiTi), it is still not possible to overcome this problem. The removal of pulp tissue, dentine debris, and bacteria using ultrasonic irrigation is much more effective than hand irrigation (Lee et al, 2004). During the ultrasonic irrigation of the root canal, the energy of the activated ultrasonic file will be transferred to the irrigation fluid in the root canal. This energy can create an acoustic micro-streaming and/or cavitation (Ahmad et al,1987; Roy et al, 1994). Two kinds of cavitation can occur: *stabile* cavitation and *transient cavitation* (Roy et al, 1994). The stabile cavitation consists of bubbles that resonate with the vibration pattern of the irrigation liquid. Around these bubbles an acoustic micro-streaming occurs. During ultrasonic irrigation, the fluid in the canal demonstrates a marked flowing pattern in which the bubbles pulsate strongly and can implode very rapidly, causing shockwaves. This phenomenon is called *transient cavitation* and results in a very violent acoustic micro-streaming in the root canal. The cleaning effect of this transient cavitation is impressive. When an ultrasonic file vibrates freely in a liquid, there is a clear vibration pattern with visible nodes and antinodes (Ahmad et al,1987) (Figs 36 and 37). Files of differing thickness have these nodes and antinodes in various places, but the file tip always shows the greatest displacement and is probably responsible for the coronally directed flow generated by the vibrating file. The nodal and antinodal pattern is the same for a straight or curved file.

The tapered form of the root canal has an influence on the effectiveness of the removal of dentine debris during ultrasonic irrigation (Lee et al, 2004; Van der Sluis et al, 2005a). In a canal prepared with a master file size 20, taper 0.10, more dentine debris can be removed than when a master file size 20, taper 0.08 or taper 0.06 is used. Passive ultrasonic irrigation (PUI) is most effective when the file has sufficient space to vibrate freely. This should take place after the root canal has been shaped and the file can then oscillate freely within the root canal without touching or cutting the canal wall. Should the file make contact with the canal wall during PUI, this will weaken the acoustic micro-streaming. In a curved canal, PUI is effective when the file is preshaped.

A smooth tip used during PUI is just as effective as a cutting file (Van der Sluis et al, 2005b). In addition, the tip (Fig 38) has the advantage that it will not change the shape of the preparation, and perforation of the apical part of the root canal can be avoided.

Sodium hypochlorite (NaOCl)

When Sodium hypochlorite (NaOCl) is used during ultrasonic irrigation, the treatment is more effective than when water is used as the sole irrigant (Van der Sluis et al, 2006). NaOCl is a powerful antibacterial agent, which is capable of dissolving organic tissue. The ability of NaOCl to dissolve tissue depends on direct contact between the irrigation solution and the substrate. Due to the acoustic micro-streaming and/or cavitation that occur during the ultrasonic irrigation, pulp tissue and dentine debris will be spread around the root canal, which then increases the contact area with the NaOCl solution. Additionally, the temperature of the NaOCl solution rises due to the ultrasonic agitation, thereby increasing the tissue solubility. This has the result that an ultrasonically activated 2.5% NaOCl

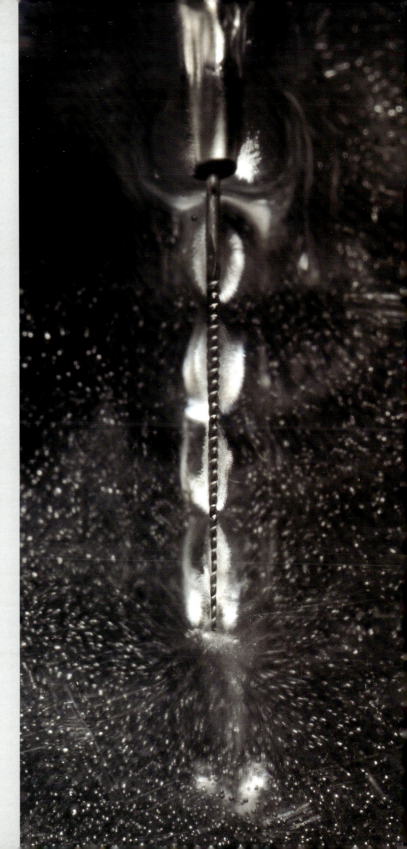

Fig 37 This figure perfectly illustrates the nodal and antinodal pattern around the tip.

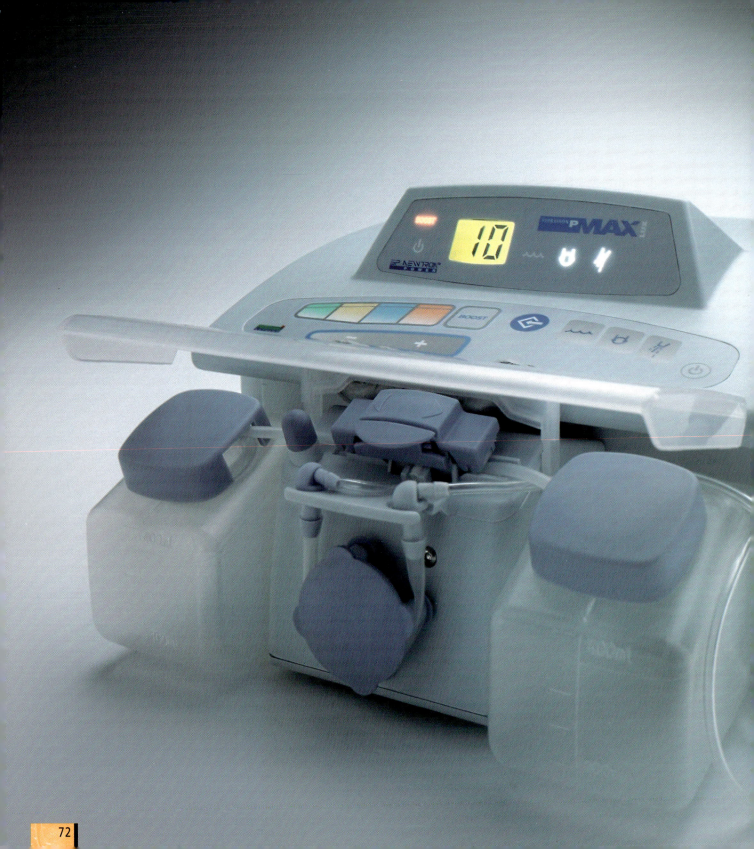

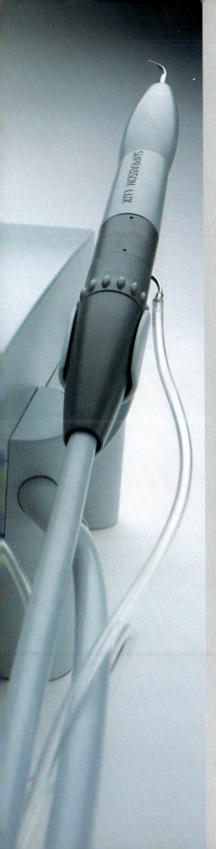

solution produces a comparable solubility tissue effect similar to a manually applied 5% solution. The physical properties of NaOCl are different from water, which can influence the transmission of energy by ultrasonics. In contrast to pure water, NaOCl is an aqueous suspension of a salt. Bubbles, especially the smallest ones formed in a solution, tend to be more numerous and are less prone to coalesce than bubbles in pure water (Leighton, 1994). Since the smallest bubbles are more numerous, the acoustic micro-streaming will be different and may even be more powerful.

Another explanation is that gas (eg, chlorine) present in the solution will dissolve in the bubbles during cavitation and the subsequent oscillations of the bubbles will then depend on the concentration of this dissolved gas, the temperature of the liquid, and the small amounts of surface active impurities (Brenner et al, 2002). This in turn influences the acoustic micro-streaming.

It is important that the NaOCl solution is refreshed during the root canal treatment, since it becomes ineffective following the reaction with pulp tissue, bacteria, or dentine debris. Within certain limits, the volume of the NaOCl solution and the application method does not seem to have a major influence on the cleaning effect of PUI. Syringe application of 2 mL NaOCl after 1 minute PUI, repeated three times, has the same effect as 3 minutes PUI with 50 mL continuous flow of NaOCl (Van der Sluis et al, 2006). A recent study showed that three sequences of 20 seconds PUI alternating with syringe delivery of 2 mL 2% NaOCl, during a total PUI of 1 minute, was as effective as three contiguous sequences of 1 minute PUI (Van der Sluis et al, 2006).

A much-heard objection against the use of a NaOCl solution in the reservoirs of an ultrasonic machine is that the accumulation of corrosive products and sodium salts would clog up and even corrode the pipes transporting the fluid in the machine. It is therefore important that after the use of a NaOCl solution, the machine, pipes, and handpiece are flushed with demineralized water. With careful maintenance and with use of concentrations of NaOCl no higher than 5%, most of the current equipment functions successfully.

Effectiveness of PUI in curved canals and anatomic structures in the root canal system that are difficult to reach

Ultrasonic irrigation is very effective in cleaning oval canals as well as an isthmus between two canals, whereas files and syringe delivery of the irrigant are, in these situations, unable to clean effectively (Goodman et al, 1985). In oval canals and during the isthmus cleaning, it is recommended to have the file vibrate in the direction of the greatest diameter of the root canal or in the direction of the isthmus. In this way, the pulp tissue, dentine debris, and bacteria are effectively removed. Ultrasonic irrigation is significantly more effective than syringe delivery of the irrigant in curved canals.

Ultrasonic versus sonic

Ultrasonic instruments work with a frequency of at least 25,000 Hz. In addition to these ultrasonically operating instruments, there are also so-called sonic instruments (such as the Sonic Air of Micro-Mega), which use a lower frequency of 1,000 to 6,000 Hz. Both types of instruments have a similar construction: The file is permanently connected to the (ultra)sonic motor at an angle of 60 to 90 degrees with respect to the long axis of the handpiece. The vibration pattern of the ultrasonic files, however, is different from that of sonic instruments. Ultrasonic files have numerous nodes and antinodes across the length of the instrument, while the sonically operated files have a single node near the attachment of the file and one antinode at the tip of the file. Sonic instruments produce an elliptic, lateral movement, similar to that of the ultrasonic files. When the movement of the sonic file is hampered in such a way that the lateral movement disappears, the remaining vibration will be longitudinal. This longitudinal movement could theoretically be favorable for the effectiveness of the irrigation. However, this has not been confirmed by research.

Four articles have appeared in which sonic and ultrasonic irrigation were compared. Two studies showed that ultrasonic irrigation was significantly more effective in removing dentine debris from the root canal than the sonic irrigation. Two other studies showed no significant differences (Walker & del Rio, 1989). It should be noted that in one of the latter

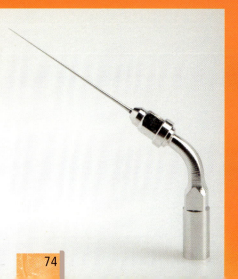

Fig 38 Smooth ultrasonic irrigation tip (ESI/EMS).

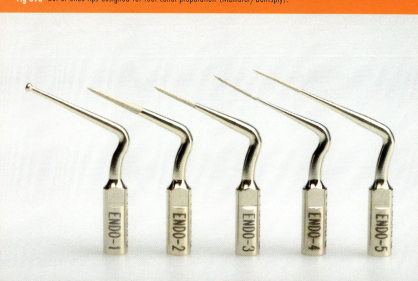

Fig 39a Set of endo-tips designed for root canal preparation (Maillefer/Dentsply).

studies, PUI was not applied, while in the other study treatment was performed in curved canals without mentioning whether the files were preshaped. It can possibly be concluded from these studies that ultrasonic irrigation is more effective in removing dentine debris from the root canal than sonic irrigation.

In summary, PUI is more effective than syringe delivery of the irrigant or sonic irrigation. NaOCl is the most effective irrigant during PUI. It is recommended to use PUI for 1 minute per canal in three sequences of 20 seconds, alternating with three sequences of syringe irrigation of 2 ml NaOCl.

Removal of posts, broken files, and other obstacles from the root canal

Ultrasonics can prove useful for the removal of all kinds of instruments from root canals. When removing a post, ultrasonics can break the cement between the post and the root canal using a thick tip (Figs 39a and 39b). To facilitate manipulation of the post, initial removal of cement or dentine from the coronal part of the root canal can be performed with long, thin preparation tips (Fig 40). The post can subsequently be extracted or unscrewed from the root canal. The threads visible on the radiograph may indicate which direction the post can be unscrewed. However, ultrasonics have little effect when the post is sealed with an adhesive cement.

There are many tips specifically designed for the removal of obstacles from the root canal, such as hardened cement, broken files, and silver points. A surgical

Fig 40 Tips specifically designed for the removal of broken instruments (Maillefer/Dentsply).

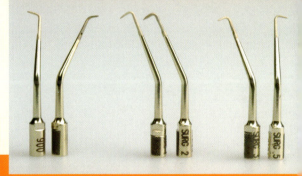

Fig 41 Tips specifically designed for apical surgery (Maillefer/Dentsply).

Fig 39b Comparable set of endo-tips produced by Satelec.

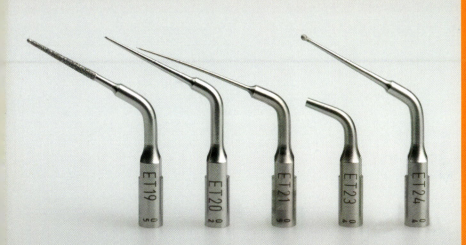

microscope is required, since direct vision of the root canal is important when working with these instruments. Ultrasonic vibrations of the tip easily loosen hard steel instruments due to the stiffness of the material. NiTi instruments are more flexible, making ultrasonics less effective. Furthermore, these NiTi instruments can sometimes easily disintegrate following contact with an ultrasonic tip, which can also be an advantage during removal.

These ultrasonic tips are easily damaged and cannot be used with high-power settings. It is therefore important to use the settings advised by the manufacturer. Preclinical training with the tips is advised and can be achieved simply by practicing on extracted teeth. The removal of broken instruments is time consuming, especially when the instrument is broken apical to a curve in the root canal. Furthermore, it is important to realize that broken instruments can be removed but always at the expense of removing of too much dentine. Under these circumstances, the therapy produces more damage than the original problem. Due to excessive undermining, the tooth may easily fracture. In addition, instrument fracture has a relatively small impact on the outcome of endodontic treatment. When teeth with and without fractured instruments were compared, the survival rate of teeth showing a initial periapical radiolucency was 87% versus 93%, while in vital teeth the results were 92% versus 94.5%.

Periapical surgery
The problem during periapical surgery is that the field of vision is limited, posing problems for ease of instrumentation. The conventional handpieces and drills are relatively large compared to the ultrasonic tips and often hamper visual access to the work area.

When the surgical microscope is used, vision is improved, but specially designed instruments are required. Ultrasonic tips are small, which enable them to be directed with precision when a surgical microscope is used. The tips can have different coatings and be placed at different angles to facilite manipulation, allowing the operator to work within the apex of the root canal. Furthermore, small apical preparations can be made parallel to the longitudinal axis of the root (Fig 41). With these tips, accurate preparation of the isthmus running between two canals can be made.

Condensing gutta-percha
Ultrasonic spreaders are a useful aid for warmed, lateral condensation and vertical compaction of gutta-percha. The ultrasonic vibrations and the heat generated lead to a higher density of the laterally condensed root canal filling and equal density when compared to a System B spreader (Van der Sluis et al, 2006).

Improving access to the root canal
With special tips, hidden and obliterated access to canal entrances can be improved (Figs 39a and 39b). Use of narrow tips makes it possible to obtain a good view of the base of the pulp chamber during preparation. The tips are generally used for this purpose without the water cooling.

Distribution of cement in the root canal
The application of a cement in the root canal is important for the quality of the filling. Prior to applying the gutta-percha, the entire root canal should be covered with cement, which is frequently difficult to accomplish. The ultrasonic vibrating file may provide a solution to this problem.

Fractures after ultrasonics

There are contradictory reports concerning the occurrence of dentine microcracks after the use of ultrasonic tips following peri-apical surgery or removal of posts and/or instruments. The occurrence of these microcracks is usually connected to the use of high-power settings. It is therefore recommended to avoid exceeding the power advised by the manufacturer.

Summary

In current endodontic practice, an ultrasonic device is indispensable, not only for cleaning the root canal, but also for nonsurgical re-treatments and periapical surgery. In general dental practice, an ultrasonic device that is suitable for both periodontal and endodontic purposes will definitely be a major asset to the practitioner.

CONCLUSION

It is clear that ultrasonic instruments are here to stay, since nowadays dentists are required to spend more time and attention to the health of the periodontal tissues.

Mechanical scalers appear to work just as well as hand instruments for the removal of plaque, calculus, and endotoxins. Ultrasonic scalers, used at low to medium power, seem to cause less damage to the root surface than manual or sonic scalers. Furcations are more easily accessible with the use of mechanical instruments than with hand instruments, due to the narrow shape of the tips. It is not clear if roughness of the root surface is more or less pronounced following the use of mechanical or manual scalers. It is also unclear if roughness of the root surface affects wound healing in the long-term. Periodontal scaling and root planing is directed toward the complete removal of calculus, but complete removal of root cementum does not have to be the focus of periodontal therapy. Studies have determined that endotoxins are only slightly absorbed to the root surface; they can easily be removed by the light overlapping strokes of an ultrasonic scaler.

One disadvantage of mechanical scalers is the production of contaminated aerosols. This is true for all rotary instruments that require a spray coolant. Extra caution is needed to maintain good infection control with the use of mechanical scalers. At present, the addition of certain antimicrobial agents to the liquid coolant during ultrasonic instrumentation appears to have minimal clinical advantages. Allowing the patient to rinse with an antimicrobial agent prior to the ultrasonic treatment (eg, chlorhexidine) does seem to reduce the bacterial load of the aerosol.

To conclude, mechanical scalers should be a part of the profession's armamentarium and deserve to play a significant role during the different phases of periodontal therapy and endodontic treatment.

REFERENCES

Ahmad, M., Pitt Ford, T.R. & Crum, L.A. (1987) Ultrasonic debridement of root canals: Acoustic streaming and its possible role. *Journal of Endodontics,* **13**, 490–499.

Balamuth, L. (1952) Method and means for removing material for a solid body. *U.S. Patent* No 2, 580,716.

Bandt, C.L. (1964) Bacteremias from ultrasonic and hand instrumentation. *Journal of Periodontology,* **35**, 214–215.

Brenner, M.P., Hilgenfeldt, S. & Lohse, D. (2002) Single bubble sonoluminescence. *Reviews of modern physics,* **74**, 425–484.

Catuna, M.C. (1953) Sonic energy. *Annals of Dentistry,* **12**, 100.

Croft, L., Nunn, M., Crawford, L., Holbrook, T., McGuire, M., Kerger, M. & Zacek, G. (2003) Patient preference for ultrasonic or hand instruments in periodontal maintenance. *International Journal of Periodontal and Restorative Dentistry,* **23**, 256–273.

Curie, J. & Curie, P. (1880) Sur l'électricité polaire dans les cristaux hémièdres à faces inclines. *Comptes Rendus de l'Académie des Sciences,* **91**, 383.

Darby, M.L. & Walsh, M. (2003) Dental Hygiene Theory & Practice, 2nd edition. W.B. Saunders, Philadelphia.

Dragoo, M.R. (1992) A clinical evaluation of hand and ultrasonic instruments on subgingival debridement: With modified and unmodified ultrasonic inserts. *International Journal of Periodontics and Restorative Dentistry,* **12**, 310–323.

Drisko, C.L. (1993) Scaling and root planning without overinstrumentation: Hand versus power-driven scalers. *Current Opinion in Periodontology*, **1**, 78–88.

Drisko, C.L. & Lewis, L. (1996) Ultrasonic instruments and antimicrobial agents in supportive periodontal treatment and retreatment of recurrent or refractory periodontitis. *Periodontology 2000,* **12**, 90–115.

Gagnot, G., Prigent, H., Darcel, J., Michel, J-F. & Cathelineau, G. (1999) Effects of composite ultrasonic tips on implant abutments. Study in vitro. *Journal de Parodontologie & d'Implantologie Orale*, **18**, 393–399.

Goodman, A., Reader, A., Beck, M., Melfi, R. & Meyers, W. (1985) An in vitro comparison of the efficacy of the step-back technique versus a step-back/ultrasonic technique in human mandibular molars. *Journal of Endodontics,* **11**, 249–256.

Joule, J.P. (1847) On the effects of magnetism upon the dimensions of iron and steel bars. *London. Philosophical Magazine*, Series **3**, 30, 76.

Laird, W.R. & Walmsley, A.D. (1991) Ultrasound in dentistry. Part 1—Biophysical interactions. *Journal of Dentistry,* **19**, 14–17.

Lee, S.J., Wu, M.K. Wesselink, P.R. (2004) The efficacy of ultrasonic irrigation to remove artificially placed dentine debris from different-sized simulated plastic root canals. *International Endodontic Journal,* **37**, 607–612.

Leighton, T.G. (1994) The acoustic bubble. Academic Press, New York.

Leon, E.L. & Vogel, R.I. (1987) A comparison of the effectiveness of hand scaling and ultrasonic debridement in furcations as evaluated by differential dark-field microscopy. *Journal of Periodontology,* **58**, 86–94.

Listgarten M.A. & Ellegaard, B. (1973) Electron microscopic evidence of a cellular attachment between junctional epithelium and dental calculus. *Journal of Periodontal Research,* **8**, 143–150.

Lumley, P.J. & Walmsley, D. D. (2002) Sonics and ultrasonics in endodontics. In: Color Atlas of Endodontics. editor, W.T. Johnson, W.B. Sauders, Philadelphia.

Martin, H. (1976) Ultrasonic disinfection of the root canal. *Oral Surgery, Oral Medicine, Oral Pathology,* **42**, 92–99.

Miller C.S., Leonelli, F.M. & Latham, E. (1998) Selective interference with pacemaker activity by electrical dental devices. *Oral Surgery, Oral Medicine, Oral Pathology,* **85**, 33–36.

Nosal, G., Scheidt, M.J., O'Neal, R. & Van Dyke, T.E. (1991) The penetration of lavage solution into the periodontal pocket during ultrasonic treatment. *Journal of Periodontology,* **62**, 554–557.

Pameijer, C.H., Stallard, R.E. & Hiep, N. (1972) Surface characteristics of teeth following periodontal instrumentation: A scanning electron microscope study. *Journal of Periodontology,* **43**, 628–633.

Position Paper, Sonic and Ultrasonic Scalers in Periodontics (*2000) Journal of Periodontology,* **71**, 1792–1801.

Postle, H.H. (1958) Ultrasonic cavity preparation, *Journal of Prosthetic Dentistry,* **8**, 153–160.

Rateitschak-Pluss, E.M., Schwarz, J.P., Guggenheim, R., Duggelin, M. & Rateitschak, K.H. (1992) Non-surgical periodontal treatment: Where are the limits? An SEM study. *Journal of Clinical Periodontology,* **19**, 240–244.

Roy, R.A., Ahmad, M. & Crum, L.A. (1994) Physical mechanisms governing the hydrodynamic response of an oscillating ultrasonic file. *International Endodontic Journal,* **27**, 197–207.

Ruhling, A., Schlemme, H., Konig, J., Kocher, T., Schwahn, C. & Plagmann, H.C. (2002) Learning root debridement with curettes and power-driven instruments. Part I: A training program to increase effectivity. *Journal of Clinical Periodontology,* **29**, 622–629.

Schroer, M.S., Kirk, W.C., Wahl, T.M., Hutchens, L.H. jr., Moriarty, J.D. & Bergenholz, B. (1991) Closed versus open debridement of facial grade II molar furcations. *Journal of Clinical Periodontology,* **18**, 323–329.

Sculean, A., Schwarz, F., Berakdar, M., Romanos, G.E., Brecx, M., Willerhausen, B. & Becker, J. (2004) Non-surgical periodontal treatment with a new ultrasonic device (Vector-ultrasonic system) or hand instruments. *Journal of Clinical Periodontology,* **31**, 428–433.

Setcos, J.C. & Mahyuddin, A. (1998) Noise levels encountered in dental clinical and laboratory practice. *International Journal of Prosthodontics*, **11**, 150–157.

Smart, G.J., Wilson, M., Davies, E.H. & Kieser, J.B. (1990) The assessment of ultrasonic root surface debridement by determination of residual endotoxin levels. *Journal of Clinical Periodontology,* **17**, 174–178.

Street, E.V. (1959) A critical evaluation of ultrasonics in dentistry. *Journal of Prosthetic Dentistry*, **9**, 132–141.

Timmerman M.F., Menso L., Steinfort J., van Winkelhoff A.J., Van der Velden U. & Van der Weijden, G.A. (2004) Atmospheric contamination during ultrasonic scaling. *Journal of Clinical Periodontology,* **31**, 458–462.

Torfason, T., Kiger, R., Selvig, K.A. & Egelberg, J. (1979) Clinical improvement of gingival conditions following ultrasonic versus hand instrumentation of periodontal pockets. *Journal of Clinical Periodontology,* **6**, 165–176.

Van der Avoort, P.G.G.L. & Endstra, L. (1999) Professionele gebitsreiniging. Een handboek over instrumenten en instrumentatietechnieken. Bohn Stafleu Van Loghum, Houten.

Van der Sluis, L.W.M., Wu, M.K. & Wesselink, P.R. (2005a) The efficacy of ultrasonic irrigation to remove artificially placed dentine debris from human root canals prepared using instruments of varying taper. *International Endodontic Journal,* **38**, 764–768.

Van der Sluis, L.W.M., Wu, M.K. & Wesselink, P.R. (2005b) A comparison between a smooth wire and a K-file in removing artificially placed dentine debris from root canals in resin blocks during ultrasonic irrigation. *International Endodontic Journal,* **38**, 593–596.

Van der Sluis, L.W.M., Wu, M.K. & Wesselink, P.R. (2006) The influence of volume, type of irrigant and flushing method on removing artificially placed dentine debris from the apical root canal during passive ultrasonic irrigation. *International Endodontic Journal* in press.

Versteeg, P.A. & Van der Weijden G.A. (2002) Ultrasoon geupdatet, *Tandarts Praktijk*, **5**, 2–8.

Waerhaug, J. (1956) Effect of rough surfaces upon gingival tissue. *Journal of Dental Research,* **35**, 323–325.

Walmsley, A.D., Laird, W.R.E. & Williams, A.R. (1988) Dental plaque removal by cavitational activity during ultrasonic scaling. *Journal of Clinical Periodontology*, **15**, 539–543.

Wilkins, E.M. (1999) Clinical Practice of the Dental Hygienist, 8th edition. Lippincott Williams & Wilkins, Philadelphia.

Zinner, D.D. (1955) Recent ultrasonic dental studies including periodontia without the use of an abrasive. *Journal of Dental Research*, **34**, 748–749.

SUGGESTED READING

Badersten, A., Nilveus, R. & Egelberg, J. (1984) Effect of nonsurgical periodontal therapy. II. Severly advanced periodontitis. *Journal of Clinical Periodontology,* **11**, 63–67.

Hallmon, W.W. & Rees, T.D. (2003) Local anti-infective therapy: Mechanical and physical approaches. A systematic review. *Annals of Periodontology,* **8**, 99–114.

Petersilka G.J. & Flemmig T.F. (1999) Subgingival root surface treatment using sonic- and ultrasonic scalers. *Parodontologie,* **3**, 233–244.

Trenter, S.C. & Walmsley, A.D. (2003) Ultrasonic dental scaler: associated hazards. *Journal of Clinical Periodontology,* **30**, 95–101.

Tunkel, J, Heinecke, A. & Flemmig, T.F. (2002) A systematic review of efficacy of machine-driven and manual subgingival debridement in the treatment of chronic periodontitis. *Journal of Clinical Periodontology,* **29** (suppl), 72–81.

ACKNOWLEDGMENTS:
Translation of this book from Dutch into English has been made possible through the generosity of Satelec and the Clinic for Periodontology Utrecht.

Europe Média Duplication s.a.s., 53110 Lassay-les-Châteaux
N° 17129 - Imprimé en France
Dépôt légal : Mars 2007

차례 |  TABLE OF CONTENTS

SIJO ✿ SHIJO ✿ GOSHIJO

THE BELOVED CLASSICS OF KOREAN POETRY ON EVERYTHING POLITICAL

FROM THE MID-JOSEON ERA

(1441~1689)

LUMPY
PUBLISHING

What is SIJO ✻ SHIJO ✻ GOSHIJO?

Sijo, the correct pronunciation being "shijo," is a form of Korean poetry that emerged during the Goryeo time period. It may be likened to an artistic expression of Confucian philosophy, since it was first and foremost the Confucian scholars who had embraced this poetic style (as opposed to the Buddhist style, a rival ideology during those times). The poem itself is quite short. It is limited to three lines with a mere 14-16 syllables to a line. However, that is not to say that there cannot be longer sijos, because there are sijos which are surprisingly long. Nevertheless, be it long or short, sijo, especially the "goshijo" (the classical sijo as opposed to the modern sijo), masterfully captures the mindset, the worldview, and the narrative of the Confucius scholars of the age—the nobility who are also referred to as the "yangban."

Sijo is a form of poetry, yes. Yet, it is important to note that people not only recited it but also sang it. Sijo presented via music is called "shijo chang" (ch+ah+ng). Of course, not all sijos are accompanied by music and not all sijos need to be sung. People do memorize and recite them just as is. No music, period. However, the classical sijo, also called "goshijo," have been sung and have received recognition as the slowest song in the world. It is easy to see why. Each syllable is drawn out and **stretched** out as the vocalist pitches up and down and showcases a gamut of vocal techniques. Mind you, the vocalist does not steal the whole show. Instruments such as the drum accompany the singer, playing in time and in perfect harmony with the emotional vibe of the moment. Without a doubt, "shijo chang" is a unique musical expression that captures the heartbeat of a nation. The singer has put to song the shouts of joy along with the inconsolable wails of mourning and grief. That may explain why the song is so slow. It cannot be but slow when the singer is wailing and crying all the while performing.

Come on in! I'm glad that you're here. I take it that you're eager to turn the pages and step into the bygone days of Korea. But, if I may, I do want to pause you just for a moment before you do so. In truth, many beautiful poems did come out of the mid-Joseon time period. And in this book, you'll find twenty masterpieces that have found a home in the hearts of the people. However, be warned. These poems are not light and airy like a meringue. As you will soon find out, this was a turbulent time period, so much so that the poets did what they could to weather the storm that raged on and on—they bared their heavy hearts through poetry. So, do gird up your heart as the poets invite you to see the world through their eyes.

Warmly, Miss Anna

Please follow the path

as you go back in time...

S I
J O

1. WITH A SWORD AT HAND

장검을 빠혀 들고

(Nah+m), EE | Nami | 남 이 (1441-1468): Joseon 조선시대

장검을 빠혀 들고　백두산에 올라 보니

대명천지에　성진이 잠겼에라

언제나 남북풍진을　헤쳐 볼꼬 하노라

말 뜻풀이 ★
Word Study in Korean

장검을 빠혀 들고: 긴 칼을 빼어들고 |

대명천지에: 환하게 밝고 넓은 세상에 |

성진이 잠겼에라: 피비린내 나는 먼지가 자욱하구나 |

남북풍진을: 전쟁의 먹구름을

(남: 일본의 왜구, 해적들)

(북: 오랑캐인 여진족들)

호
기
가

ho-(G+ee)-gah
A Song of Valiance

장검을
(jah+ng)-(g+au+m)-(eu+l)
a long sword

빠혀 들고
(PP+ah)-(h+y+au) (d+eu+l)-(g+oh)
unsheathing and holding it

백두산에
(beh+k)-doo-(sah+n)-eh
on Mt. Baekdu

올라 보니
(oh+l)-lah boh-nee
I went up and saw

대명천지에
deh-(m+y+au+ng)-(ch+au+n)-jee-eh
in the wide and bright world

성진이
(s+au+ng)-jee-nee
bloody red dust

잠겼에라
(jah+m)-(g+y+au+t)-seh-rah
is soaked in it

언제나
(au+n)-jeh-nah
oh when

남북풍진을
(nah+m)-book-poong-jin-(eu+l)
the clouds of wars and battles with the Jurchen people
(the future Qing empire) in the north the and Japanese pirates in the south

헤져 볼꼬 하노라
heh-(ch+au) (boh+l)-(GG+oh) hah-noh-rah
will I fight them off

NOW TRY TO PUT IT IN YOUR OWN WORDS!

FOR EXAMPLE:

Gripping a sword in my hand, I went up to the highest of heights of Mt. Baekdu.
But what should I see but swells of blood blanketing the vast expanse!
Oh, when would I ever cleave asunder all the enemies rolling in like the clouds?

CONTEMPLATION:

A deep desire to fend for and protect one's country

여진족
(오랑캐)
The Jurchens

일본 왜구
(해적)
The Japanese
Pirates

음하하하!!! MWAHAHAH!!!
조선을 먹으로 가자!
Let's go get her (Joseon)!

MEET THE POET: (Nah+m), EE (the grandson of King Tejong; a brave young general falsely incriminated and slain)

General Nahm EE was a great general. Yes, he was young, but he was brave nonetheless and highly spirited. At the age of 26, he was subduing rebellions and fighting off the Jurchens in the north and fighting the Japanese pirates in the south. He was a noble, young warrior who was highly favored by King Sejo (the 7th king of Joseon). However, not everyone regarded him favorably. Yu Ja-(Gwah+ng) and his jealous eyes spied on him, hoping to find a way to falsely accuse him of treachery. As luck would have it, he had the ears of the next king, King Ye-Jong, who also felt uneasy about General Nahm EE. For one, the young general was a threat to his throne as he was a member of the royal family—the grandson of King Tejong (the 3rd king of Joseon). Yu Ja-(Gwah+ng) flipped the narrative of (Nah+m) EE's patriotism and accused him of treason. And sadly, this story unfolded into a tragedy, for this innocent young general was sentenced to a cruel death. He was only 27.

백두산 돌

칼 갈아 없애고

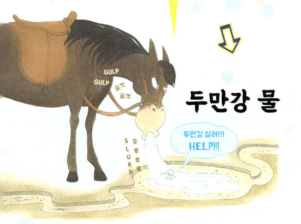

두만강 물

말 먹여 없애리

Clenching the Fist!!!

2. I WILL GRIND MY SWORD ON MT. BAEKDU

백두산 돌 칼 갈아 없애고

(Nah+m), EE | Nami | 남 이 (1441-1468): Joseon 조선시대

후세에 뉘라서 대장부라 하리요

남아 나이 이십에

나라 평정 못할진대

Word Study in Korean
남아 나이 이십에: 남자 (사나이) 나이 스물에 | 나라 평정 못할진대: 나라를 평탄하게 못한다면 | 후세에 뉘라서: 훗날에 누가

호
기
가

ho-(G+ee)-gah
A Song of Valiance

백두산 돌
(beh+k)-doo-(sah+n) (doh+l)
the rock called Mt. Baekdu

두만강 물
doo-(mah+n)-(gah+ng) mool
the waters of the Tumen River

남아
(nah+m)-ah
a man

후세에
hoo-seh-eh
in later generations

칼 갈아
(kah+l) gah-rah
(by) sharpening the sword

말 먹어
(mah+l) (m+au)-(g+y+au)
(by) watering the horse

나이 이십에
nah-ee ee-shib-eh
when at the age of twenty

뉘라서
(noo+ee)-rah-(s+au)
who would he be to them

없애고
(au+b)-seh-(g+oh)
I will get rid of it

없애리
(au+b)-seh-ree
I will get rid of it

나라 평정
nah-rah (p+y+au+ng)-(j+au+ng)
to give peace to the country

못할진대
(moh+t)-(hah+l)-jin-deh
if he cannot

대장부라 하리요
deh-(jah+ng)-boo-rah hah-ree-yoh
that they would call him a virtuous leader of a man

NOW TRY TO PUT IT IN YOUR OWN WORDS!

FOR EXAMPLE:

I'll grind my sword on Mt. Baekdu, grinding the mountain down to the very roots!

I'll water my horse in the Tumen River, letting the river run dry!

Listen, all of you in your twenties!

If you, in your twenties, cannot secure peace for your nation, you, sir, are a loser.

Why would anyone shower you with honor as a great leader?

CONTEMPLATION:

A deep desire to be someone great for one's country

혜성이라... Why, a falling star...
옛 것은 뒤로하고

새로운 것을 맞이하라.
그런 징조가 아니었던가?
It's a sign, they say.
"Out with the old,
in with the new."

오호!
Gotcha!

이 말을 엿들은
간신 유자광
The eavesdropping villain,
Yoo Ja-Gwang

MEET THE POET: (Nah+m), EE (the grandson of King Tejong; a brave young general falsely incriminated and slained)

Poems have the power to stir up emotions and thoughts. Unfortunately for General Nahm EE, his had the power to stir up trouble. His poem, this very one along with a passing comment he made about a shooting star, was used against him, incriminating him for treason. Jealous colleagues, especially Yoo Ja-(Gwah+ng), framed him as a traitor to the crown and as one who plotted to seize the throne for himself. Of course, this was far from the truth! Yes, the young general was somewhat hotheaded and outspoken. And yes, he had a mind of his own with regards to political affairs. Yet, he was not treacherous, only ambitious, daring, and full of youthful vigor and passion for greatness. He desired to live up to the virtues of a great man and serve his country well. However, his dreams were cut short as he was betrayed by his own country and countrymen. His story was all the more tragic because no one stood up for his innocence. Maybe the shooting star was a sign of his own passing—a sign that foretold of the fall of a great man.

3. PLEASE STAY. WHY DO YOU INSIST ON LEAVING? 있으렴 부디 갈다

King (S+au+ng)-(Joh+ng) | King Seong-Jong | 성 종 (1457-1494): Joseon 조선시대

있으렴

부디 갈다

아니 가든

못할소냐

무단히

싫더냐

an honorable government position

남의 말을 들었느냐

그래도 하

애닯구나

가는 뜻을

일러라

말 뜻풀이 ★ Word Study in Korean

있으렴: 물러가지 말고 (고향으로 돌아가지 말고) 내 옆에 있으려무나 | 부디 갈다: 꼭 가겠느냐? 굳이 가야지 되겠느냐? |

아니 가든 못할소냐: 가지 않으면 안 되겠느냐? | 무단히 싫더냐: 여기가 진정 싫어서 그러느냐? 벼슬도 싫더냐? |

남의 말을 들었느냐: 남이 너에게 뭐라고 하더냐? 너를 힘들게 하는 사람이 있었던 것이냐? |

그래도 하 애닯구나: 그래도 몹시 슬프구나, 매우 서운하구나 | 가는 뜻을 일러라: 그래도 꼭 가야만 된다면 그 이유를 내게 말하거라

있으렴
its-(s+eu)-(r+y+au+m)
please stay

부디 갈다
boo-dee (gah+l)-dah
do you truly have to go?

아니 가든
ah-nee gah-(d+eu+n)
for you to not go

못할소냐
(moh+t)-(hah+l)-soh+(n+yah)
would it not be possible

무단히
moo-(dah+n)-hee
intensely

싫더냐
shil-(t+au)-(n+yah)
you don't care for it (the honorable position)?

남의 말을
(nah+m)-eh (mah+l)-(eu+l)
what others are saying about you

들었느냐
(d+eu+l)-(au+d)-(n+eu)-(n+yah)
have you heard

그래도
(g+eu)-reh-doh
still

하
hah
truly very

애닲구나
eh-(dah+l+b)-goo-nah
sorrowful I feel

가는 뜻을
gah-(n+eu+n) (DD+eu)-(s+eu+l)
why you wish to go

일러라
il-(l+au)-rah
please tell me

NOW TRY TO PUT IT IN YOUR OWN WORDS!

FOR EXAMPLE:

Please stay. Why do you insist on leaving? Could you please reconsider? Must you go?

Why do you want to go? Did you hate your post that much? Or, heaven forbid, did somebody talk behind your back?

Whatever the case may be, I'm utterly miserable. Please, do tell me why you really mean to go away.

CONTEMPLATION:

A king's plea to a faithful and devoted subject who desires retirement

MEET THE POET: King (S+au+ng)-(Joh+ng) (the 9th 👑 of Joseon)

What is a king? Behind all the fineries and the royal regalia is a man who, like everybody else, seeks true friendship and trust that goes beyond the man-made constraints of position and class. However, for kings such friendships are rare though loyal subjects there be many. Hence the agony of losing such a friend. King (S+au+ng)-(Joh+ng) knew this so well. When official Yoo Hoh-In presented his desire to retire from his post (for it was a filial duty to take care of his ageing mother), the king was distraught no doubt. He tried to persuade him to stay, but it was to no avail. The friend's mind was made up. He wanted to go back home. Therefore, the king did what he could do for his friend. He prepared a farewell party and composed this heartfelt poem just for him. Indeed, such was a man beneath the crown. Genuine friendship was a luxury even for kings.

4. YET UNTIL THE DAY WHEN A DUCK'S STUBBY LEGS

오리의 짧은 다리

Kim, Goo | 김 구 (1488-1543):
Joseon 조선시대

오리의 짧은 다리   학의 다리 되도록애

검은 가마귀   해오라비 되도록애

항복 무강하사   억만세를 누리소서

중종: 조선 제11대 왕
King Jung-Jong, the 11th King of Joseon

말 뜻풀이 ★
Word Study in Korean

되도록애: 될 때까지 | 해오라비: 해오라기의 옛말, 백로 |

항복 무강하사: 끝없이, 언제까지나 복을 누리시어 | 억만세: 억만 년

VOCABULARY

오리의
oh-ree-eh
a duck's

짧은 다리
(JJ+ah+l)-(b+eu+n) dah-ree
short legs

학의 다리
(hah+g)-eh da-ree
a crane's legs

되도록애
(doh+eh)-doh-(roh+g)-eh
until they become

검은 가마귀
(g+au+m)-(eu+n) gah-mah-(goo+ee)
a black crow

해오라비
heh-oh-rah-bee
an egret

되도록애
(doh+eh)-doh-(roh+g)-eh
until it becomes

항복 무강하사
(hah+ng)-(boh+g) moo-(gah+ng)-hah-sah
may you receive heaven's blessings forever

억만세를
(au+g)-(mah+n)-seh-(r+eu+l)
for a million year

누리소서
noo-ree-soh-(s+au)
savor, enjoy

CONTEMPLATION:

"I love what you are doing as our king. May you live forever to see all of your visionary dreams fulfilled."

NOW TRY TO PUT IT IN YOUR OWN WORDS!

FOR EXAMPLE:

Until that day. . .the day when a duck's stubby legs become as long as those of the crane's...

Until that day. . .the day when a black crow becomes an egret...

May you ever live until that day!

Yes, for thousands and for millions of years, may you live on forever blessed by the heavens.

자네가 보기에도 뭔가 이상하지 않나? Is it only me or do you also smell some mischief afoot?

MEET THE POET: Kim, Goo (an offical, scholar, writer/poet)

Kim Goo was one of Joseon's foursome* who knew how to paint with words. He was also a brilliant scholar who was passionate about learning. One day, he was up late studying when the king, during one of his moonlit strolls, heard him reading aloud from an empty study hall, the Ok-Dang. Pleased and delighted to find a true scholar-at-heart, the king invited himself over and honored him with a bottle of wine which he poured out himself. Kim Goo was deeply touched. When prompted by the king, he improvised this piece on the spot and rendered it before him. By all appearances, the poem seems quite silly. Who has ever heard such well-wishes? Can a duck beget longer legs, or can a crow become an egret? Better yet, can the king live forever? It may sound ludicrous and offensive, insulting even. However, at the light of the moment, the poem was well-received and the heart of the poet well-appreciated. Joong-Jong (Jung-Jong) was a king who actively sought to purge the court of corruption by encouraging revolutionary reforms. In light of the events, the poet was gushing out his respect for the king, praising him for his enlightened mind and his progressive ways. To say the least, he wasn't swooning about the wine.

*Joseon's foursome: Ahn Pyung-Dae-Goon, Yang Sa-Aun, Han Ho-Deung, and Kim Goo

찌릿! a leering glare

학 Crane

백로 해오라기 Egret

5. EVEN IN THE COLD OF WINTER

삼동에 베옷 입고

Joh, Shik | Jo, Shik | 조 식 (1501-1572): Joseon 조선시대

임금님께서 승하 하셨다네... ㅠㅠ
한 번 뜨고는 저물어 가는 인생이라...
I hear that the king had passed away...
Ah, the coming and the going of life...

삼동에 베옷 입고   암혈에 눈비 맞아

구름 낀 볕뉘도   쬔 적이 없건마는

서산에 해 지다 하니   눈물겨워 하노라

말 뜻풀이 ★
Word Study in Korean

삼동에: 한겨울의 석 달 동안 (나라가 혼란스러운 세월동안) |

베옷 입고: 베로 지은 옷을 입고 (벼슬하지 않고) |

암혈에: 바위와 굴에 (제대로 된 집도 없이 굴에서 운둔생활을 하면서 |

구름 낀 볕뉘도: 구름 사이에 낀 햇볕도 (임금님의 작은 은혜도, 은총도) |

볕뉘도 쬔 적이 없건마는: 벼슬을 함으로 임금님의 은총을 입어 본 적이 없지마는 |

서산에 해 지다 하니: 임금님께서 승하하셨다고 하니 (중종왕, 조선 11대 왕)

삼동에	베옷 입고	암혈에	눈비 맞아
(sah+m)-(doh+ng)-eh	beh-(oh+t) ip-goh	(ah+m)-(h+y+au+l)-eh	noon-bee mah-jah
in the three cold winter months	wearing clothes made of flax	in the rocky cave	with falling rain and snow

구름 낀 별뉘도	쬔 적이	없건마는
goo-(r+eu+m) (GG+in) (b+y+au+l)-(noo+ee)-doh	(JJ+wen) jau-(g+ee)	(au+b)-(g+au+n)-mah-(n+eu+n)
a sunshine covered by the clouds	to have basked in it	I never did

서산에	해 지다 하니	눈물겨워 하노라
(s+au)-(sah+n)-eh	heh jee-dah hah-nee	noon-mool-(g+y+au)-(w+au) hah-noh-rah
on the western mountains	hearing that the sun has set	tears are welling up in my eyes

NOW TRY TO PUT IT IN YOUR OWN WORDS!

FOR EXAMPLE:

Even in the dead cold of winter, clothed only in flax, I dwell in the caves, weathering the rain and the snow.
I have never basked in the sunshine, not even in the ones shadowed by the clouds.
Still, my eyes welled up with tears when I heard that the sun has set over the western horizon.

CONTEMPLATION:

Sadness over the passing of the king (King Jung-Jong, the 11th king of Joseon)

나는 학문에 정진하며 인재를 키우는데에 몰두하리라. 이것이 님을 향한 나의 충성이라.
The studies that I do... The raising up of the next generation of scholars... I do them out of loyalty to my king.

MEET THE POET: Joh, Shik (a wise and learned hermit who refused to enter into the king's services)

Joh Shik. He was a brilliant man, a true teacher, and a scholar of Confucianism. As many praised his name, Joseon's kings often summoned him to the court with the promise of an honorable position. However, Joh Shik refused. Again and again he refused. He did come before the throne and bowed before the king ONCE, but for him that was one time too many. The story goes that he left the king's presence like the wind, leaving in the majesty's hands words of advice on how to deal with rebellions and advice on the merit of being a scholar-of-a-king. Was Jo Shik unpatriotic? In all cases, he rather did appear to be a surly subject. But was he? No. On the contrary. Regardless of what others whispered about him, here was a man who was loyal to his king in his own way. Of course, he did choose the life of a hermit over the life of an honored official (the "sunshine" in the poem). However, the court being rife with corruption and strife, he decided that he could serve the king best by doing what he did best: studying and laboring in learning all the while teaching and discipling many in his cave. Indeed, here was a man with his own take on deep-set loyalty and service to the king.

6. DEAR BIRDS, DON'T SORROW OVER THE FADING BLOOMS

꽃이 진다 하고   (Soh+ng), Soon | Song, Soon | 송 순 (1493-1588): Joseon 조선시대

꽃이 진다 하고   새들아 슬허 마라

바람에 흩날리니   꽃의 탓 아니로다

가노라 희짓는 봄을   새워 무엇하리요

을사사화 (1545)   을사년에 있었던 많은 선비들의 학살 | 12세의 명종이 조선의 제 13대 왕으로 즉위하던 해에 당파싸움에서 예기치 않게 갑이 된 어머니 문정왕후와 그녀의 세력이 을이 되어버린 당파를 몰살시켰던 사건

The 4th Literati Purge of 1545-
When twelve-year-old (M+yau+ng)-(Joh+ng) ascended the throne as the 13th king of Joseon, his mother assumed power as the acting regent as the king was yet too young to rule. Given all power, she took it upon herself to wipe out the rivaling political party which was led by Confucian scholars.

말 뜻풀이 ★ word Study in korean   새들아 슬허 마라: 새들아 슬퍼하지 말아라 | 바람에 흩날리니: 모진 바람을 못이겨 흩어져 날리는 것이니 |

가노라 희짓는 봄을: 떠나는 것이 화가나 꽃들을 휘젓는 봄을 | 새워 무엇하리요: 샘하고 미워한들 무슨 소용이 있겠느냐

꽃이
(GG+oh)-chee
the flowers

진다 하고
jin-dah hah-goh
saying that they are falling

새들아
seh-(d+eu+l)-ah
dear birds (the people of the land)

슬허 마라
(s+eu+l)-(h+au) mah-rah
do not be sad

바람에
bah-(rah+m)-eh
it's the wind

흩날리니
(h+eu+t)-(nah+l)-lee-nee
since it is scattering it

꽃의 탓
(GG+oh)-cheh (tah+t)
the flower's fault

아니로다
ah-nee-roh-dah
it is not

가노라
gah-noh-rah
because it has to go away

희짓는
(h+eu+ee)-jit-(n+eu+n)
storming and throwing a fit

봄을
(boh+m)-(eu+l)
of spring

새워
seh-(w+au)
be envious

무엇하리요
moo-(au+d)-hah-ree-yoh
why be

NOW TRY TO PUT IT IN YOUR OWN WORDS!

FOR EXAMPLE:

Dear birds, don't be sad to see the flowers fade away.
It's the windy gale that's blowing them away. Hence, the flowers are falling due to no fault of their own.
It's just Spring throwing a tantrum because it sees that its days are coming to an end.
So, why let your heart be troubled about this passing season of rage?

CONTEMPLATION:

Sadness over the tragic execution of countless scholars of the court
all the while believing that this too will pan out in due time

휴~ 줄을 잘 서서
다행이다.
I'm glad that I sided with
the winning side.

사람파를 내치거라!!!
다 죽어라!!!
KILL! KILL! KILL!
Kill all of those scholars!

어린 명종왕의 어머니: 문정왕후 (8년간 수렴청정함)
The mother of King (M+yau+ng)-(Joh+ng)
Queen Moon-(Jau+ng) who reigned as regent for 8 years

MEET THE POET: (Soh+ng), Soon (a much respected offical and scholar)

How the tables have turned! When King In-Jong (the 12th 👑) mysteriously died just after a short reign of 8-9 months (He was only 30 years old), his twelve-year-old half brother suddenly found himself the next king of Joseon. This was indeed a serendipitous event to ONE of the two rival factions. For years and years, the court was a scene of an unfolding drama of intrigue and conspiracy. Two rival factions had each lined up behind one of the princes (and the respective mothers of the princes), hoping that their prince would be the next king. But when King In-Jong suddenly died, the faction of the deceased king suddenly found themselves cornered and hemmed in. Overnight, the Queen Consort Moon-(Jau+ng) [Moon-Jung], the mother of the young king, became the acting Regent, and she became very powerful as she took on all the liberties of a king. And what was to be her first order of the day? KILL, KILL, and KILL! Called the 4th literati (the scholars) purge (Eul-Sa Sa-Hwa), she put to the sword everyone who had withstood her faction. (Soh+ng) Soon grieved to see so many men of learning swept away by this terrible purge. However, as a seasoned politician, he knew that this storm too, like so many other storms before, would pass away and be no more.

7. YOU KNOW THAT PINE TREE THAT WAS HEWN DOWN

엊그제 벤 솔이

Kim, In-Hoo | 김인후 (1510-1560):
Joseon 조선시대

벽서사건과 정미사화

명종 (조선의 13대 👑) 즉위 2년 정미년에 (1547) 어린 명종 뒤에서 수렴청정하는 문정왕후를 비판하는 벽서가 전라도 양재역에서 발견되었다. 을사사화의 뿌리가 아직 남은거라고 하여 많은 선비들이 에매한 혐의로 죽임을 당했다.

The Writing on the Wall and the Literati Purge of 1547

Two years into the reign of young king Myeong-Jong, people found writings on a wall that criticized the queen, the active regent of Joseon. That scribbling in the far away province of Jeolla-Do so infuriated the queen that she again put to the sword many Confucian scholars in order to wipe out that political group entirely. All were innocent.

엊그제 벤 솔이 낙락장송이 아니런가

적은덧 두던들 동량재 되리러니

어즈버 명당이 기울면 어느 나무가 버리랴

말뜻풀이 ⭐ word Study in Korean | 엊그제 벤 솔이: 엊그제 배어 버린 소나무가 | 낙락장송이 아니런가: 곧게 자란 훌륭한 소나무가 아니었던가? (친구 임형수) |

적은덧 두던들: 잠깐 동안이라도 더 두었더라면 | 동량재 되리러니: 기둥이 될 만한 제목이었을 텐데, 대들보가 될 만한 훌륭한 인재가 되었을텐데 |

이즈버: 아~ | 명당이 기울면: 나라가 기울어지면 (명당: 좋은 묏자리g훌륭한 건물g임금의 조현을 받는 정전g조정g나라) |

어느 나무가 버티랴: 어느 나무로 버티어 내야 하는가? 어느 나무가 (기울어지는) 나라를 받치겠는가?

엊그제
(au+d)-(g+eu)-jeh
a few days ago

벤 솔이
ben (soh+l)-ee
the pine tree that was cut down

낙락장송이
(nah+ng)-(rah+g)-(jah+ng)-(soh+ng)-ee
a grand and stately pine tree

아니런가
ah-nee-(r+au+n)-gah
wasn't it so

적은덧
jau-(g+eu+n)-(dau+d)
even for a little while

두던들
doo-(d+au+n)-(d+eu+l)
if it were left alone

동량재
(doh+ng)-(r+yah+ng)-jeh
a mighty pillar

되리러니
(doh+eh)-ree-(r+au)-nee
it could have become

어즈버
au-(j+eu)-(b+au)
but alas

명당이 기울면
(m+yau+ng)-(dah+ng)-ee (g+ee)-ool-(m+y+au+n)
if the 'kingdom' were to collapse

어느 나무가
au-(n+eu) nah-moo-gah
which tree

버티랴
(b+au)-tee-(r+yah)
will support it

a fine site for a grave→a fine building→the part of the palace designated for
ceremonies and rituals→the government→the kingdom

더는 못 버티겠어!!!
I can't hold this up for long!!!

조선 Joseon

후~
Sigh~

누구
없소?
Anyone?

CONTEMPLATION:

Despair over the unwarranted and pointless killing of an excellent scholar and friend

NOW TRY TO PUT IT IN YOUR OWN WORDS!

FOR EXAMPLE:

Remember that pine tree that was hewn down a few days ago?

Don't you agree that it was a magnificent tree?

Were it left alone even for a short while, it would have served as a mighty pillar.

But alas... What tree would now hold up the kingdom if it were to list and cave in?

MEET THE POET: Kim, In-Hoo (a dear friend of Im Hyung-Soo who was framed and killed)

It was Queen Moon-(Joh+ng) [Moon-Jung] unleashing her fury yet again! In a remote village far, far away, a nameless writer scribbled on a wall a scathing remark about the queen. It read, "The queen and her corrupted faction are ruining our nation! Are you going to stand back and do nothing?" When the queen was told about the graffiti, let's just say that she wasn't over the *moon* about it. It was a mere two years ago that she had purged the court, killing off the rival faction, putting more than a hundred scholars to the sword. And trembling with rage, she did not hesitate to do so again. There was no evidence or proof to condemn any of the scholars. Many of them were highly respected and honored by the people. They were ones who would have served the nation well. Nonetheless, hundreds of officials were ruthlessly cut down as traitors and as enemies of the kingdom. Im Hyung-Soo was one of the great trees that fell during this bloody purge. And when he died, many were horrified and grieved beyond words for he was an exceptional man, gifted in mind, and noble in his ways. He was only 43. Kim In-Hoo wrote this poem lamenting his friend's needless death.

8. ONE FROSTY WINDY DAY

풍상이 섞어친 날에

(Soh+ng), Soon | Song, Soon | 송 순 (1493-1588): Joseon 조선시대

아! AH!

풍상이 섞어친 날에

갓피온 황국화를

금분에 가득 담아

옥당에 보내오니

도리야 꽃이온양 마라

님의 뜻을 알괘라

Plum Flower
복숭아꽃
오얏꽃
Peach Flower

말풋풀이 ★ Word Study in Korean

풍상이 섞어친 날에: 바람이 불고 서리가 내린 날에 |

금분: 귀한 화분 | 옥당: (홍문관) 조선의 행정기관 및 연구기관 |

도리야: 빨리 지는 복숭아 꽃과 오얏꽃 (자두꽃) |

꽃이온양 마라: 꽃인 척도 하지마라 |

님의 뜻을: 임금님의 뜻을 | 알괘라: 알겠구나

퀴즈 겸 미션
QUIZ & MISSION
짐의 깊은 뜻을 헤아려
노래를 지어올리거라.
Figure out my message
and submit it to me
in a poetic sijo format.

풍상이 섞어친 날에
poong-(sah+ng)-ee (s+au)-(GG+au)-chin (nah+l)-eh
on a windy day with showering sleet

갓피온
(gah+t)-pee-(oh+n)
freshly blossomed

황국화롤
(h+w+ah+ng)-gook-(h+w+ah)-(r+eu+l)
golden chrysanthemums

금분에
(g+eu+m)-boo-neh
in a precious (golden) vase

가득 담아
gah-(d+eu+g) (dah+m)-ah
in abundance

옥당에
(oh+k)-(dah+ng)-eh
to the Ok-Dang

보내오니
boh-neh-oh-nee
were delivered

도리야
doh-ree-yah
plum and peach flowers

꽃이온양 마라
(GG+oh)-chee-(oh+n)-(yah+ng) mah-rah
don't even act like flowers

님의 뜻을
nim-eh (DD+eu+d)-(ch+eu+l)
the king's heart

알괘라
(ah+l)-(go+eh)-rah
I understand

NOW TRY TO PUT IT IN YOUR OWN WORDS!

FOR EXAMPLE:

One frosty and windy day,
Sumptuous blooms of yellow chrysanthemums were delivered to the Ok-Dang,
the golden vase brimming with blooms.
Dear plum flowers and peach flowers, don't even think about calling yourself flowers.
I believe I understand why the king has sent them.

CONTEMPLATION:
The virtues of a loyal official

그대가 짐의 마음을 읽었노라!
You read my mind!

엄지 척!
THUMBS UP!

MEET THE POET: (Soh+ng), Soon (a much respected offical and scholar)

One icy fall day, (Soh+ng) Soon, a much respected government official, was working in the main office (the Ok-Dang) when the chrysanthemums arrived. The blooms were from King (M+yau+ng)-(Joh+ng) [Myeong-Jong] himself (Jo-seon's 13th king), and with them came a two-fold instruction: to discern the meaning and present the meaning through a song (or sijo/shijo). This quiz-like mission was impossible! How could anyone surmise the king's thoughts, let alone his intended meaning? It was then that (Soh+ng) Soon raised his hand, volunteering to answer the king's behest. Chrysanthemums faithfully bloom notwithstanding the sleet and icy cold winds. Could it be that the golden vase (methaphor for the king) was seeking the company of such flowers? Officials who are men of integrity and honor, officials who are steadfast in their fidelity? Far be it that his subjects would be like the peach and plum flowers whose petals are quick to fall away. When (Soh+ng) Soon sang out his answer, the king was pleased and thrilled indeed. Did (Soh+ng) Soon receive a reward for this feat? The story does not tell us, but that golden vase (along with those chrysanthemums) would have been a kingly gift indeed, don't you think?

9. I AM OLD, IT'S HIGH TIME I RETIRE!

늙었다 물러가자   (Soh+ng), Soon | Song, Soon | 송 순 (1493-1588): Joseon 조선시대

이 님을: 왕을, 임금님을 | 어디로메 가잔 말고: 어디로 가잔 말인가? | 너란: 너는

늙었다
(n+eu+l)-(g+au+d)-(DD+ah)
I am old

물러가자
mool-(l+au)-gah-jah
I should retire

마음과
mah-(eu+m)-(goo+ah)
with my heart

의논하니
(eu+ee)-(noh+n)-hah-nee
I hold a talk

이 님을 버리고
ee nim-(eu+l) (b+au)-ree-goh
Leaving this ONE

어디메로
au-dee-meh-roh
to where

가잔 말고
gah-(jah+n) (mah+l)-goh
are you trying to go?

마음아
mah-(eu+m)-ah
Heart

너란 있거라
(n+au)-(rah+n) it-(g+au)-rah
you remain behind

몸만
(moh+m)-(mah+n)
only my body

물러가리라
mool-(l+au)-gah-ree-rah
shall go away

NOW TRY TO PUT IT IN YOUR OWN WORDS!

FOR EXAMPLE:

"I am too old. It's high time I retire," I moaned to my heart.

"Now just where do you think you're going and that without your king?" the heart retorted.

To this I replied, "Heart, why don't you stay behind. Only my body shall go away."

마마...
Your Highness...

제가 남아서 마마를
모시겠나이다...
I will stay behind to serve you...

CONTEMPLATION:

An internal debate of a faithful and devoted subject who is facing retirement

MEET THE POET: (Soh+ng), Soon (a much respected offical and scholar)

It is true that (Soh+ng) Soon cut quite a figure among all his associates. He was not only highly intelligent but also good-natured, making him well-liked and respected even by warring political parties. Devoted to the king, not to mention highly competent and capable, (Soh+ng) Soon was honored again and again. He was even granted the second highest rank a court official could reach. Of course, by that time, he was not the young man that he used to be, and his eighty-year-old bones told him so; he had served the king for fifty years! He knew that it was high time for him to retire, but being the loyal servant that he was, he felt conflicted at the same time. How could he ever resign from his service to the king? Then came a wonderful idea! His heart can stay behind and remain serving at the court! Though he leaves, his heart will forever go on serving the king. Little wonder that he was favored by the king!

10. OH, WHAT TO DO! TO DO SO TO THE NOBLE TIMBERS

어와 동량재를
(J+au+ng), (Ch+au+l) | Jeong, Cheol | 정 철 (1536-1593): Joseon 조선시대

어와: 아! (안타까움과 한탄의 감탄사) | 동량재: 건축물의 대들보감; 마룻대와 들보로 쓸 만한 재목 | 동량재를 저리하여 어이할꼬:

훌륭한 재목들을 (나라를 바로 이끌 인재들을) 베어 버리니 이를 어찌할까 | 헐뜯어: 하도 인재들을 헐뜯고 모함해서 |

기운 집에: 기울어진 집을 앞에 놔두고, 무너져가는 나라를 놔두고 | 의논도 하도할샤: 당쟁들의 의논이 (시비와 말싸움이) 많기도 많구나 |

뭇 목수: 여러 목수 (뭇: 여러명) | 고자 자 들고: 고자와 자 (고자: 목수가 먹줄을 칠 때 쓰는 먹고자=먹통) (자: 줄자) |

허둥대다 말려나다: 능력없어 허둥대기만 하다가 일을 그만 두려는가?

어와
au-wah

oh (with a groan)

동량재를
(doh+ng)-(r+yah+ng)-jeh-(r+eu+l)

timbers perfect for pillars and colonnades

저리하여
(j+au)-ree-hah-(y+au)

to do so (in that manner)

어이할꼬
au-ee-(hah+l)-(GG+oh)

what to do

헐뜯어
(h+au+l)-(DD+eu)-(d+au)

due to reviling and harrassment

기운 집에
(g+ee)-oon jee-beh

in additon to a house listing

의논도
(eu+ee)-(noh+n)-doh

of discussions (disputes)

하도할샤
hah-doh-(hah+l)-shah

they are doing endlessly

뭇 목수
moot (moh+g)-soo

a number of carpenters

고자 자 들고
goh-jah jah (d+eu+l)-goh

holding an ink chalk-liner and a ruler

허둥대다
(h+au)-doong-deh-dah

after fumbling
and bungling about

말려는다
(mah+l)-(l+y+au)-(n+eu+n)-dah

are they giving up

NOW TRY TO PUT IT IN YOUR OWN WORDS!

FOR EXAMPLE:

Oh dear~ What in tarnation did they do to the mighty timbers???!!!
The house is listing, run down by their constant bashing,
and yet here they are bickering and squabbling!
Look at all these carpenters with their ink chalk-liners and rulers!
But wait! Why, they are leaving! Are they really done for the day?
How can they be done when all they did was fumble and bungle about the whole day long?

CONTEMPLATION:

exploring the factional divisions in the court and mourning over the tragic fate of many virtuous scholars

PUNCH! PUNCH! 팍팍!!!

PUNCH! PUNCH! PUNCH! 팍팍팍!!!

아야 아퍼~ 아프다고 ㅠㅠ OUCH!!! It hurts~ Did you hear me?

나라를 어지럽히는 당파싸움
Factional Divide that Destroys a Nation

MEET THE POET: (J+au+ng), (Ch+au+l) (a famous statesman and poet who also goes by the penname, Sohng-Gahng)

Doubtless, factional divide was like a thick black cloud hanging over Joseon, the court and the kingdom. Of course, this division was nothing new in the political weavings of the country. From its early days, statesmen had knitted themselves into parties, each vying for more power, influence, and supremacy over the others. However, everything took a turn for the worse and came to a head during the mid-Joseon era. Countless scholars, gifted and abled officials of the court, lost their lives due to false accusations and false reports crafted by evil men. Naturally, the carpenters in the poem allude to such political schemers whose intentions are indeed far from noble. They care not about repairing the listing house, the dilapidating kingdom of Joseon (not to say that they are qualified for the job). And feeling their very position and place threatened by principled and just men, they would strike them down by any means, their favorite being the arts of chicanery. (J+au+ng) (Ch+au+l) himself did not escape the net laid by treacherous men, the scheming conspirators and conniving agents in the court. He was exiled and died a lonely death as a wayfarer. Hence this poem mourns the fate of the kingdom and of so many other great men, his included.

11. OH, THAT I COULD DRAW OUT MY HEART

내 마음 베어내어 (J+au+ng), (Ch+au+l) | Jeong, Cheol | 정 철 (1536-1593): Joseon 조선시대

내 마음 베어내어   저 달을 만들고자

구만리 장천에   번듯이 걸려 있어

고운님 계신 곳에 가   비추어나 보리라

말뜻풀이 ★
Word Study in Korean

내 마음 베어내어: (임금님을 그리워하는) 내 마음을 베어내서 |

저 달을 만들고자: 저 달을 만들고 싶구나 | 구만리 장천에: 아득히 높고 넓고 푸른 하늘에 |

번듯이 걸려 있어: 번듯하게 떠 있으면서, 훤히 떠 있으면서 |

고운님: 임금님 (선조 임금님, 조선의 14대 👑) |

고운님 계신 곳에 가: 임금님 계신 궁궐로 가 |

비추어나 보리라: 훤히 내 마음을 비추고 싶구나

내 마음
neh mah-(eu+m)
my heart

베어내어
beh-au-neh-au
cutting it out

저 달을
(j+au) (dah+l)-(eu+l)
that moon

만들고자
(mah+n)-(d+eu+l)-goh-jah
I would like to make

구만리 정천에
goo-(mah+n)-lee (jah+ng)-(ch+au)-neh
in the wide and endless blue expanse

번듯이
(b+au+n)-(d+eu)-shee
clearly and properly

걸려 있어
(g+au+l)-(l+y+au) it-(s+au)
hanging

고운님
goh-oon-nim
my king

계신 곳에 가
(g+eh)-shin goh-seh gah
going towards where he is

비추어나 보리라
bee-choo-au-nah boh-ree-rah
I would like to shine

NOW TRY TO PUT IT IN YOUR OWN WORDS!

FOR EXAMPLE:

Oh, that I could draw out my heart and mold it into a moon...
I would have hung it beautifully on the wide blue expanse,
So that it would go and shine its light above my beloved king...

CONTEMPLATION:

A confession of a subject's devotion towards his king

어라...
넌 누구니?
Wait a minute...
Who do you claim to be?

나? 난 정철이의 마음 ♥
Me? I'm Jaung Chaul's heart ♥

MEET THE POET: (J+au+ng), (Ch+au+l) (a famous statesman and poet who also goes by the penname, Sohng-Gahng)

For the most part, Joseon's kings were not deified or worshipped as a god, but they were to be served with the utmost devotion and loyalty. And what do you think was held as one of the central virtues in the teachings of Confucianism? What do you know! Absolute loyalty to the king! Needless to say, many subjects did fully embrace and embody this virtue. Here in this poem is (J+au+ng) (Ch+au+l) baring his aching longing for his liege, King (Sau+n)-Joh [Seon-Jo] (the 14th 👑 of Joseon). He was a good king especially in the onset of his reign. Notably, he garnered the respect of many scholars as he tried to mend the wounds caused by the previous four purges on the literati, the scholarly politicians of Confucianism. He honored those who were martyred for the hapless cause and swiftly dealt out justice to the corrupt men who had schemed those purges. The land did enjoy a moment of peace during the early part of his reign. However, political factions quarreled still and an even a bigger threat of danger loomed on the horizon as the Japanese hungrily eyed the peninsula basking in all out peace. As there was no standing army, Joseon was a sitting duck. (Jau+ng) (Chau+l) probably wrote this poem during the chaos of the Im-Jin War with Japan. The king was far away and in hiding.

12. AS MOONLIGHT SHINES DOWN UPON THE HANSAN ISLAND

한산섬 달 밝은 밤에

Yi, Soon-Shin | Yi, Sun-Sin | 이순신 (1545-1598): Joseon 조선시대

한산섬 달 밝은 밤에　수루에 혼자 앉아

긴 칼 옆에 차고　깊은 시름 하는 적에

어디서 일성호가는　남의 애를 끊나니

말 뜻풀이 ★
Word Study in Korean

한산섬: 한산도, 거제도와 통영 사이에 있는 섬,
통영에서 뱃길로 30분 |
수루에: 적의 움직임을 살펴보는 높은 망루에 |
일성호가는: 갈대잎 피리 (대나무 피리) 에서 울려오는 애잔한 곡조는;
(일성) 한 곡조, (호가) 갈대잎을 말아 만든 피리 |
남의 애를 끊나니: 남의 마음을 애달프게 한다

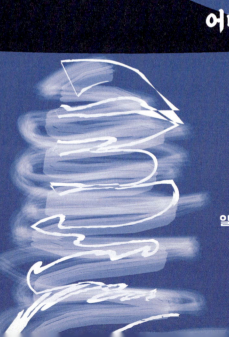
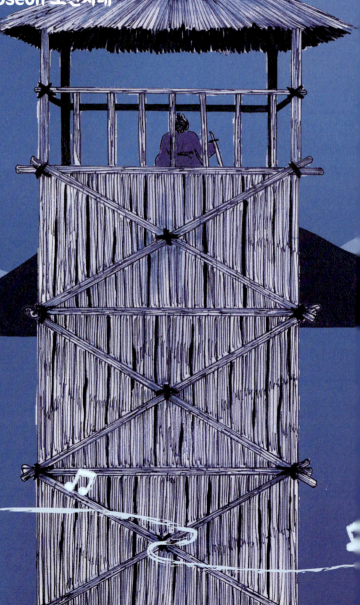

한산섬
(hah+n)-(sah+n)-(s+au+m)
in an island in Hansan

달 밝은
(dah+l) (bah+l)-(g+eu+n)
when the moon was shining bright

밤에
(bah+m)-eh
at night

수루에
soo-roo-eh
on a lookout tower

혼자 앉아
(hoh+n)-jah (ah+n)-jah
sitting alone

긴 칼
(g+een) (kah+l)
(with) a long sword

옆에 차고
(y+au)-peh cha-goh
beside me

깊은 시름
(g+eep)-(eu+n) shee-(r+eu+m)
deep anguish

하는 적에
hah-(n+eu+n) (j+au)-(g-eh)
as I was having

어디서
au-dee-(s+au)
from where (that I know not)

일성호가는
il-(s+au+ng)-hoh-gah-(n+eu+n)
the tune from a leaf flute

남의
nah-meh
someone's

애를 끊나니
eh-(r+eu+l) (GG+eu+n)-nah-nee
it deeply agonizes the heart

CONTEMPLATION:

A deep anguish of the heart, mind, and soul

NOW TRY TO PUT IT IN YOUR OWN WORDS!

FOR EXAMPLE:

A silvery light shines down upon the island,

Here I am alone in the tower,

a sheathed sword resting beside me as I wrestle with my heart within.

But hark! I hear a plaintiff piping of a flute drifting through the trees...

Oh, how the wistful tune rends this heart with anguish...

마음이 무겁구나.
How heavy my heart is...

MEET THE POET: Yi, Soon-Shin (the greatest Korean general and admiral, the hero who saved Joseon)

General Yi Soon-Shin was well acquainted with the sorrows and the sufferings of war. He was a brave fighter and a brilliant strategist who had led the charge in more than twenty navy battles. Each victory kept Joseon safe from the invading Japanese, and each victory rekindled hope to the reeling nation. However, victories came at a cost. He saw firsthand the sacrifices of his men and of his colleagues. He witnessed the toils of the people and the tears shed for the lost loved ones. And he beheld the utter devastation and the ravages of war. As fearless and bold as he was, he still was but a man with raw emotions and a raw heart. And on a still and lonely night such as this, with the silver moon softly shining down upon the land, a plaintiff song and a silvery tune would be enough to overwhelm an already troubled soul. Imagine a heart weighed down by layer after layer of gnawing fears, hurts, and aches, and all these held at bay by a singular twine called patriotic loyalty. Such was the life of General Yi Soon-Shin. Oh, the deep anguish he must have felt. General Yi Soon-Shin gave his all for his country until the very moment that he died. He died of a gunshot wound during the epic sea battle that forever ended the Imjin War, the Battle of Noryang. He had given Joseon his all.

13. AS A FIRE HAS STARTED IN THE SPRING-GREEN MOUNTAIN

춘산에 불이 나니　Kim, (D+au+k)-(R+y+au+ng) | Kim, Deok-Ryeong | 김덕령 (1567-1596): Joseon 조선시대

활~ 활~
Fire roaring~

화르르르르~
Fire crackling~

춘산에 불이 나니　못다 핀 꽃 다 붙는다

저 뫼 저 불은　끌 물이 있거니와

이 몸에 내 없는 불이 나니　끌 물 없어 하노라

불이야!!!

IT'S A FIRE!!!

나는 결백하요!
I'm innocent!

춘산에 불이 나니: 봄이 찾아온 산에 불이 나니 (임진왜란) | 못다 핀 꽃: 피어보지도 못한 꽃들이 불에 타는구나 (싸우다 전사한 청년들) |
저 뫼 저 불은 끌 물이 있거니와: 저 산에 난 저 불은 물로 끌 수 있다만은 | 이 몸에 내 없는 불이 나니: 내 몸에는 연기도 없이 타는 불이 나니 |
끌 물 없어 하노라: (이 불을) 끌 물이 없어 안타깝기만 하는구나

춘산에
choon-(sah+n)-eh
in the spring mountain

불이 나니
bool-ee nah-nee
as a fire is burning

못다 핀 꽃
(moh+d)-dah pin (GG+oh+d)
the flowers yet to blossom

다 붙는다
dah bood-(n+eu+n) dah
are catching on fire

저 뫼
(j+au) (m+weh)
that mountain

저 불은
(j+au) bool-(eu+n)
that fire

끌 물이
(GG+eu+l) mool-ee
water to snuff out the fire

있거니와
id-(g+au)-nee wah
there is

이 몸에
ee moh-meh
on my body

내 없는
neh (au+b)-(n+eu+n)
a smokeless

불이 나니
bool-ee nah-nee
a fire is burning

끌 물 없어 하노라
(GG+eu+l) mool (au+b)-sau hah-noh-rah
I am distraught because there is no water to douse this fire
(or because there is no water that could extinguish this fire)

NOW TRY TO PUT IT IN YOUR OWN WORDS!

FOR EXAMPLE:

A fire is burning up the mountain green, (Im-Jin War with Japan)

and young blooms are caught up in the flames! (Many young soldiers have sacrificed their lives.)

Still, there is hope as there is water to douse the flames. (With valiant young men battling, this war would someday come to an end.)

However, alas, here is my body burning up in smokeless flames (I am mired in trouble as well as I have been framed and have been sentenced to death.)

with no water to extinguish this fire. (I am distressed beyond words as there is no way to attest to my innocence and live.)

CONTEMPLATION:

A cry of an innocent general just moments before his execution

MEET THE POET: **Kim, (D+au+k)-(R+y+au+ng)** (a brave young general who fought beside Admiral Yi Soon-Shin)
Here is another one in the line of great men falsely accused and killed. Kim (D+au+k)-(R+y+au+ng) was a great general and one who could have served Joseon well. Though he was young, he was known for his valiant courage and for his keen, sharp mind as a strategist. Rumors of his might spread far and wide, so much so that General Kato Kiyomasa of Japan, during the Im-Jin War, secretly hired an artist to draw a portrait of him. General Kato was not disappointed. Here indeed was a true general, brave and noble in his ways, not to mention handsome. However, life can be cruel, and it was so for this young general. After the war, he was accused of colluding with the insurgents (a coup led by Lee (Moh+ng)-Hahk) which he was sent to squash. For more than twenty days, he was cruelly interrogated and tortured in prison, and the court still argued and debated about his innocence even as his life was fading away. Here was a young general who was betrayed by the very country he deeply loved. He was only 29 when he died.

14. SINCE THE POLITICAL AFFAIRS ARE PATHETIC

시절도 저러하니

Lee, (Hah+ng)-(Boh+k) | Lee, Hang-Bok | 이항복 (1556-1618): Joseon 조선시대

시절도 저러하니   인사도 이러하다

이러하거니   어이 저러 아니하리

이렇다 저렇다 하니   한숨겨워 하노라

시절도 저러하니: 나라가/정치가 저 모양이니, 저 지경이니 | 인사도 이러하다: 사람들이 (정치인들이) 하는 모든 일이 이 꼴 이 모양이구나 |

이러하거니: (또는) 정치인들이 모두 이 꼴이니 | 어이 저러 아니하리: 나라가 어떻게 저 꼴이 되지 않을 수 있겠는가 |

이렇다 저렇다 하니: 정치가 이렇다고 해서 시비를 걸고 또는 정치인들이 저렇다고 해서 서로 싸움질만 하니 | 한숨겨워하노라: 한숨만 나오는구나

시절도
shee-(j+au+l)-doh
because the world of politics

저러하니
(j+au)-(r+au)-hah-nee
is like that

인사도
in-sah-doh
the politicians and their doings also

이러하다
ee-(r+au)-hah-dah
are like this

이러하거니
ee-(r+au)-hah-(g+au)-nee
because the politicians are like this

어이 저러 아니하리
au-ee (j+au)-(r+au) ah-nee-hah-ree
how can the world of politics be but that

이렇다
ee-(r+au)-tah
because they point their finger to the world of politics

저렇다 하니
(j+au)-(r+au)-tah hah-nee
because they point their finger to the politicians

한숨겨워 하노라
(hah+n)-soom-(g+y+au)-(w+au) hah-noh-rah
I just heave a sigh

NOW TRY TO PUT IT IN YOUR OWN WORDS!

FOR EXAMPLE:

Pathetic are the political affairs and thus pathetic are the politicians.

Indeed, how can you have one without the other?

Pathetic they be together and pathetic they go together. Hand in hand they go.

Yet here they are pointing their fingers at each other.

This is altogether pathetic! What can I do but heave a sigh...

CONTEMPLATION:

Dismay as he observes the infighting and divisions within Joseon's political system

MEET THE POET: **Lee, (Hah+ng)-(Boh+k)** (a great statesman, a man of excellence and integrity)

Lee (Hah+ng)-(Boh+k) is heaving sigh after sigh. How can he not? Men in service to the king, men who had vowed to be servants of the kingdom, are fighting and quarreling amongst themselves. They are banding themselves into tightly knitted groups and pitting against each other. When will they ever get a grip of themselves and serve the nation with a united front? Yet, it is easy to blame. The statemen are pointing their fingers at Joseon: "It's all because the Kingdom of Joseon is a mess!" they complain. At the same time, Joseon is pointing her finger at the statesmen: "It's all because the politicians are a mess!" it cries. No one is yielding, and no one is leading the charge to create peace and unity. Would the court ever be united? Here is Lee (Hah+ng)-(Boh+k) just sighing day after day.

철령 높은 봉에

Lee, (Hah+ng)-(Boh+k) | Lee, Hang-Bok | 이항복 (1556-1618): Joseon 조선시대

철령 높은 봉에 쉬어 넘는 저 구름아

고신원루를 비삼아 띄어다가

님 계신 구중심처에 뿌려 본들 어떠리

참 안됐구만...
How terriby sad...

딸 뜻풀이 ★ Word Study in Korean │ 철령: 강원도 회양군과 함경남도 고산국 사이에 있는 큰 고개 이름 | 고신원루를: 임금님의 저버림을 받아 곁을 떠나는 원통하고 외로운 눈물을 | 님 계신: 임금님 계신 (광해군을 말한다) | 비 삼아 띄어다가: 비로 만들어 실어다가 |

구중심처: 대궐 안 깊은 곳에 (구중궁궐: 대궐의 대문이 9 겹으로 되어 있기에 대궐을 구중이라고 불렀다.)

항복이의 소원을
들어주러 왔수다.
I'm here to make
Hahng-Bok's wish
come true.

VOCABULARY

철령 높은 봉에

(ch+au+l)-(r+y+au+ng) (noh+p)-(p+eu+n) (boh+ng)-eh

in the heights of a big hill called Chaul-Ryung

고신원루를

goh-shin-won-roo-(r+eu+l)

the bitter tears I shed for being cast aside

님 계신

nim (g+eh)-shin

where the special one is

(Gwang-Hae-Gun, the 15th king of Joseon)

쉬어 넘는

(sh+wee)-au (n+au+m)-(n+eu+n)

that rests upon it and then moves on

비삼아

bee-(sah+m)-ah

turning them into raindrops

구중심처에

goo-(joo+ng)-shim-(ch+au)-eh

deep in the palace with nine gates

tears
눈물

저 구름아

(j+au) goo-(r+eu+m)-ah

you clouds over there

띠어다가

(TT+eu+ee)-au-dah-gah

carrying them over

뿌려본들 어떠리

(PP+oo)-(r+y+au)-(boh+n)-(d+eu+l) au-(TT+au)-ree

how would it be if you were to
sprinkle them down

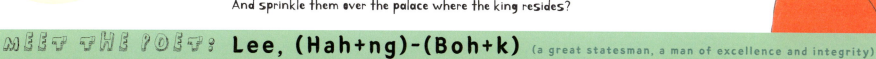

NOW TRY TO PUT IT IN YOUR OWN WORDS!

FOR EXAMPLE:

Dear clouds, yes you who have made camp on the tops of that giant knoll,

(If it's not too much to ask,)

Would you please carry my bitter tears as raindrops

And sprinkle them over the palace where the king resides?

CONTEMPLATION:

A plea of innocence

on the trek into exile

난데없이 비가
내리는군...
Rain? All of a
sudden?

MEET THE POET: Lee, (Hah+ng)-(Boh+k) (a great statesman, a man of excellence and integrity)

It was a dark time for Joseon. A dangerous storm was brewing over the crowning of the next king. As expected, such turbulent times gave rise to intrigue, division, and deep-set conflict in the court, and hardly anyone was left unscathed as they tried to tread through such volatile circumstances. Who would it be? Would it be the young son, the favorite of the late king, and by lineage, legally the crown prince—Prince (Yau+ng)-(Chah+ng) [Yeong-Chang]? Or would it be the much older son, the one who was hastily crowned as the next in line and left to guard the kingdom when the Japanese army swept into the land—Prince (Gwah+ng)-(Heh) [Gwang-Hae]? He did so much to calm the people and organize the army to fight while his father, the late king, fled for his life and hid in the northernmost province of (OO+ee)-Joo [Ui-Ju]. Yet, he was the son, more so the second son of a consort and not the queen. So, who would it be? The court was divided, knives were unsheathed, and blood was spilled in alleyways. Through the storm, Prince (Gwah+ng)-(Heh) became the king, and still the storm brewed on. Now there were talks of deposing the legal young prince and his queen mother, the seeds of a potential threat to the throne. Lee (Hah+ng)-(Boh+k) wanted to avoid more needless bloodshed. He tried hard to save their lives, speaking on behalf of them ardently and fervently. And for that, he was exiled. Exiled! How could this be? Yes, he was well acquainted with the bumps and bruises that come with a political life, and even those were not due to any negligence or faults of his own. But now here he was, forever cast aside and on the ride of his life, the most bumpy and bruising ride of all! How could he not but cry bitter tears?

16. YOU KNOW THIS FIGHT THAT YOU ARE PASSIONATE ABOUT?

힘써 하는 싸움

Lee, (Dau+g)-Il | Lee, Deok-Il | 이덕일 (1561-1622): Joseon 조선시대

힘써 하는 싸움 나라 위한 싸움인가

옷밥에 묻혀있어 할 일없이 싸우는다

아마도 그치지 아니하니 다시 어이하리요

말 뜻풀이 ★ word Study in korean

힘써 하는 싸움: 힘써서 하는 당쟁, 당파 싸움 ㅣ 옷밥에 묻혀있어: 좋은 옷, 좋은 밥에 겨워서, 배가 불러서 ㅣ

할 일없이 싸우는다: 할 일이 없어 싸우는구나 ㅣ 아마도 그치지 아니하니: 당파간의 싸움이 아무리해도 그쳐지지가 않으니 ㅣ

다시 어이하리요: 이제는 어떡해 해야한단 말이요, 이제 어찌하리요

힘써
him-(SS+au)
with passion

하는 싸움
hah-(n+eu+n) (SS+ah)-oom
the fight you are fighting

나라 위한
nah-rah wee-(hah+n)
for the country

싸움인가
(SS+ah)-oom-in-gah
is it a fight

옷밥에
(oh+d)-bah-beh
with clothes and food

묻혀있어
mood-(h+y+au)-id-(s+au)
being full and satisfied

할 일없이
(hah+l) il-(au+b)-(s+au)
as you have nothing else to do

싸우는다
(SS+ah)-oo-(n+eu+n)-dah
you fight

아마도
ah-mah-doh
I guess, I perceive

그치지 아니하니
(g+eu)-chee-jee ah-nee-hah-nee
as it stops not

다시 어이하리요
dah-shee au-ee-hah-ree-yoh
what could be done, what to do

NOW TRY TO PUT IT IN YOUR OWN WORDS!

FOR EXAMPLE:

You are fighting hard and earnestly so. But if you don't mind me asking,

Are you truly fighting on behalf of the kingdom?

Well-fed and well-clothed,

you are fighting because you have nothing better to do!

But alas, the fight shows no signs of abating.

Oh, what to do, what to do?

CONTEMPLATION:

A criticism of the incessant infighting

내 이러지도 저러지도 못하는구나!!!
I'm stuck between a rock and a hard place!!!

뭐라?!!
What did you just say?!!

네 이놈!
YOU WEASEL!

MEET THE POET: Lee, (Dau+g)-Il (a statesman turned general who fought alongside General Yi Soon-Shin during the Im-Jin War)

Lee (Dau+k)-Il was tired. He was tired of factional divisions, tired of the constant bickering and contention in the court, and tired of men who call themselves statesmen but were doing nothing but argue. Without question, the kingdom of Joseon was in a dismal state. The six years of the Im-Jin War with Japan deeply battered and bruised the land and its people. It would take time to heal the nation and build it up again. It would take human resources, not to mention good leadership, to further strengthen the nation and revamp the military. Undoubtedly, the kingdom needed unity in the court and, most of all, officials who would devote their time and energy on behalf of Joseon. However, such time and energy were wasted on intense infighting and squabbling for more power. As for the king (King Seon-Jo, the 14th 👑), he found himself helplessly stuck in between and powerless. Yet, unfortunately for Joseon, the situation went from bad to worse. Kings changed but factional divisions remained, poisoning the virtue of the political system. Little wonder that Lee (Dau+k-Il) was tired. Dispirited and dejected, the general retired from the political arena during the turbulent reign of Prince (Gwah+ng)-(Heh) [Gwang-Hae] and spent the rest of his days composing poem after poem (28 poems in all) about the evils of factional divide. This was one enemy that Joseon never got to beat.

17. DEAR SAMGAK MOUNTAIN

가노라 삼각산아

Kim, (Sah+ng)-(Hoh+n) | Kim, Sang-Heon | 김상헌 (1570-1652): Joseon 조선시대

가노라 삼각산아   다시 보자 한강수야

고국산천을   떠나고자 하랴마는

시절이 하 수상하니   올동 말동 하여라

말 뜻풀이 ★
word Study in Korean

가노라: 나는 이제 떠나간다 |

삼각산: 서울 북쪽에 있는 명산; 세(3) 봉우리가 있는 산; 오늘의 북한산 |

한강수야: 한강; 한양을 지나 서해로 흘러가는 긴 강 |

고국산천: (고국)조상때부터 살아오던 나라+고향; (산천): 산과 강; 땅 |

하랴마는: 하겠는가마는 | 시절이 하 수상하니: 때가 하도, 매우, 어수선하니 |

올동 말동 하여라: 올지 말지; 돌아올 수 있을지 모르겠구나

(여진족 (오랑케) → 후금 → 청나라)
청나라의 제2차 침입: 병자호란
12월 28일 1636년 ~ 2월 24일 1637년

The Jurchens → Later Jin → Qing Dynasty
The 2nd Invasion of the Qing: Byeong-Ja-Ho-Ran
December 28, 1636 ~ February 24, 1637

VOCABULARY

가노라
gah-noh-rah
I am going

삼각산아
(sah+m)-(gah+g)-sah-nah
dear Samgak Mountain

다시보자
dah-shee-boh-jah
see you again

한강수야
(hah+n)-(gah+ng)-soo-yah
dear waters of the Hangang River

고국산천을
goh-goog-(sah+n)-(ch+au+n)-(eu+l)
the land of the ancestors, homeland and country

떠나고자 하랴마는
(DD+au)-nah-goh-jah hah-(r+yah)-mah-(n+eu+n)
far be it that I leave it

시절이
shee-(j+au+l)-ee
the times

하
hah
very

수상하니
soo-(sah+ng)-hah-nee
being tumultuous

올동 말동 하여라
(oh+l)-(doh+ng) (mah+l)-(doh+ng) hah-(y+au)-rah
I don't know if I could ever come back

NOW TRY TO PUT IT IN YOUR OWN WORDS!

FOR EXAMPLE:

I have to be on my way, Dear Samgak Mountain.
I will see you again someday, Dear Hangang River.
Far be it that I would want to leave my homeland,
But the times being as they are, I wonder if I am ever to return.

CONTEMPLATION:

A parting song to one's land and country

굽히지 않는 절개...
What resolute spirit...

존경스럽다.
Respectable, yes.

나도 저 어르신 존경 한다네.
I respect him as well.

A prisoner of war of the 2nd Qing/Manchu Invasion of Joseon(Byeong-Ja-Ho-Ran)

MEET THE POET: Kim, (Sah+ng)-(Hoh+n) (a statesman lauded for his patriotism and his unshakable spirit during the crisis of Byeongjahoran)

Kim (Sah+ng)-(Hoh+n) is leaving his country. He was personally sought for, alas, not as a guest of honor, but as a prisoner of war! The Qing Dynasty, the rising power in the northeast which would soon take over the Ming Empire, had attacked the Joseon peninsula yet again and had besieged the king (King In-Jo, the 16th king of Joseon) who had taken refuge at a remote fortress called Nam-Han-San-(Sau+ng) [Seong]. This time, their demands were more heavy and grave. If they had compelled Joseon to sign a brotherly pact with them, they now demanded Joseon to bow down to them as a subjugated nation. Naturally, the king was stunned and the officials outraged beyond words! However, time was of the essence for the king was hemmed in and the fortress running out of food and supplies. Should they bow down to their demands? Half of the court raised their hands to say yes. What future would there be for Joseon if the king and they themselves were killed? First bow down, then devise a plan they pleaded. However, the other half of the court declared, "Nay!" How could a king bow down? He must stay strong and fight back. Surely, the Ming Empire, Joseon's unwelcomed protectorate and oppressor, will come to their aid. King In-Jo was distressed, no doubt, but finally gave in to the enemy's demands. He bowed down before the Qing, and when he did, the Kingdom of Joseon bowed down with him. And as was the practice, many people were dragged away as slaves and as trophies of war. Kim (Sah+ng)-(Hoh+n) was one of them as he was the ringleader of the opposition.

18. ON THE DAY WE PARTED

이별하던 날에

(Hong, S+au)-(Boh+ng) | Hong, Seo-Bong | 홍서봉 (1572-1645): Joseon 조선시대

말뜻풀이 ★
word Study in Korean

이별하던 날에: 소현세자와
봉림대군과 이별하던 날에 |

피눈물이 난지 만지: 눈물 번벅이어서,
정신 없이 울어서, 경황이 없어서,
피눈물이 났었는지 안 났었는지 |

압록강 내린 물이: 압록강의 흐르는 물이 |

푸른빛이 전혀 없네: 푸른 물이 피눈물로
가려져 빨갛게 보이는구나 |

배 위에: 배 위에 서있는 |

허여 센 사공이: 머리가 허옇게 센 사공도 |

처음 보다 하더라: 세자들이 볼모로
잡혀가는 것을 처음 본다 하더라

이별하던 날에   피눈물이 난지 만지

압록강 내린 물이   푸른빛이 전혀 없네

배 위에 허여 센 사공이   처음 보다 하더라

이별하던
ee-(b+y+au+l)-hah-(d+au+n)
as we parted

날에
(nah+l)-eh
on the day

피눈물이
pee-noon-mool-ee
blood-red tears

난지 만지
(nah+n)-jee (mah+n)-jee
I don't know if I cried out or if I didn't cry out

압록강
(ah+m)-(noh+k)-(GG+ah+ng)
Am-Rok River

내린 물이
neh-rin mool-ee
the water flowing from

푸른빛이
poo-(r+eu+n)-bit-chee
of the color blue

전혀 없네
(j+au+n)-(h+y+au) (au+b)-neh
there is no trace

배 위에
beh (oo+ee)-eh
standing on the boat

허여 센 사공이
(h+au)-(y+au) (seh+n) sah-(goh+ng)-ee
a white-haired ferryman

처음 보다 하더라
(ch+au)-(eu+m) boh-dah hah-(d+au)-rah
first time seeing this he says

세자저하, 부디 강건하소서...
Your Highness, please take care of yourself...

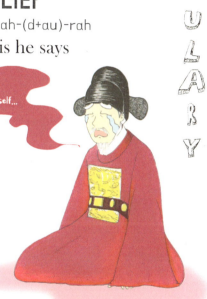

CONTEMPLATION:

The pain at seeing the princes taken away to Manchu (the Qing Empire) as hostages

NOW TRY TO PUT IT IN YOUR OWN WORDS!

FOR EXAMPLE:

As we said our goodbyes that fateful day, I may have shed crimson tears

For the river ran red without a trace of blue.

Even the old ferryman remarked that he had never seen this before.

(the river running red and/or the princes of Joseon being taken away as hostages)

MEET THE POET: **(Hoh+ng), (S+au)-(Boh+ng)** (a noble statesman and one of the members who escorted the princes to the Qing Empire)

When King In-Jo (the 16th 👑) surrendered to the Qing Empire/Manchus (the 2nd Manchu Invasion of Joseon or the Byeong-Ja-Ho-Ran, 1636), the Manchus dragged away 600,000 people as prisoners of war. Among the prisoners were hostages: the king's first born, Crown Prince Soh-Hyun [Sohyeon] (25), and his second son, Prince (Boh+ng)-Lim [Bongrim] (18)—and their wives. It was another tragic event in Korean history. Leaving the capital city of Hanseong | Hanyang, the royal entourage of 192 people wound their way up to the Amrok River | Yalu River. It took them around forty days to make it to the ferry crossing at the Am-Rok River, and, after spending a few days at the northernmost border of Joseon, it would take yet another 20 or so days to reach Shen-Yang, the capital city of the Qing Empire. But now here they were, at the bank of the river and seated on the ferry. They were leaving Joseon. Would they ever return? Would they ever come back to their homeland? Nobody knew. Official (Hoh+ng) Sau-(Boh+ng) cried and cried, bewailing the plight of Joseon and the plight of the princes. The utter humiliation of defeat was bad enough, but to have the princes taken away as hostages was another great blow. The waters of the Am-Rok River looked red to the old statesman as he was crying bitter tears.

19. HAVE WE PASSED CHEONG-SEOK-RYEONG

청석령 지나거냐

Prince (Boh+ng)-Lim→(H+yoh), (Joh+ng) |

Prince Bong-Rim→Hyo-Jong (the 17th 👑) |

봉림대군→효 종 (1619-1659): Joseon 조선시대

청석령 지나거냐   초하구는 어디메오

호풍도 참도찰사   궂은비는 무슨 일고

아무나 내 행색 그려내어   님 계신데 드리고저

말 뜻풀이 ★
word Study in korean

청석령: 만주땅 요령성 쪽에 있는 고개 | 청석령 지나거냐: 청석령을 지났느냐 | 초하구: 만주의 한 지역 이름 |

초하구는 어디메오: 초하구는 어디쯤인가 | 호풍도 참도찰사: 호지 (오랑케의 땅)에서 불어오는 바람은 차갑기 그지없구나 |

궂은비는 무슨 일고: 궂은비는 또 왠일로 내린단 말인가 |

아무나 내 행색 그려내어: (궂은 비 맞으며 오랑케의 땅으로 끌러가는) 내 이 처량한 모습을 그림으로 그려서 |

님 계신데 드리고저: 임금님께서 (아바마마께서) 계신 대궐로 보내고 싶구나

VOCABULARY

청석령
(ch+au+ng)-(sau+g)-(r+ya+u+ng)
a hill called Cheong-Seok-Ryeong in Manchuria

지나거냐
jee-nah-(g+au)-(n+yah)
have we passed

초하구는
cho-hah-goo-(n+eu+n)
a province called Cho-Ha-Gu

어디메오
au-dee-meh-oh
about where is it

호풍도
hoh-poong-doh
the Manchurian wind

참도찰사
(ch+ah+m)-doh-(ch+ah+l)-sah
is as cold as it can be

궂은비는
goo-(j+eu+n)-bee-(n+eu+n)
this bedraggling rain

무슨 일고
moo-(s+eu+n) il-goh
wherefore

아무나
ah-moo-nah
anyone

내 행색
neh heng-(seh+k)
my appearance

그려내어
(g+eu)-(r+y+au)-neh-au
I would ask to draw

님 계신데
nim (g+eh)-shin-deh
to where the king is

드리고저
(d+eu)-ree-goh-(j+au)
I would like to send it

NOW TRY TO PUT IT IN YOUR OWN WORDS!

FOR EXAMPLE:

Have we passed that hill (Cheong-Seok-Ryeong) yet? And where on earth is Cho-Ha-Gu?

Oh, how this cold Manchurian wind cut to my bones... And why, just why does it have to pour?

Were there someone to draw a picture of my miserable state, I would have posted it to the palace.

청나라? Manchuria?

배우자! Learn! Study! Analyze!

벌하자! Punish! Retaliate! Hit Back!

소현세자 Crown Prince Soh-Hyun

봉림대군 Prince Bohng-Lim

MEET THE POET: Prince (Boh+ng)-Lim (the second son of King In-Jo who succeeded him as king)

Obviously, Prince (Boh+ng)-Lim was feeling very blue. Imagine: his royal being had become a prisoner, a hostage, and that to a people whom he had despised as being barbarians. Here he was being dragged off, escorted, to say it nicely. Would he ever return? Would he even make it back alive? Dismal thoughts hounded him, and the unpredictable future stumped him. The weather did not help. The march was a cold and dreary one. The grungy rain soaked him to the bones, and the winds whipped him with the coldest possible lashes. What a reception it was! Even the Manchurian skies seemed to mock his reversal of fortune. This was too much for a hot-blooded eighteen-year-old. Prince (Boh+ng)-Lim seethed with anger. And for the rest of his life, even after his safe return home eight years later and after he ascended the throne as the next king, revenge would be the only thought that would occupy his heart and mind. He never did overcome the trauma and the humiliation of defeat.

It would be remiss if nothing was said about the Crown Prince Soh-Hyun. Unlike his younger brother, Prince Soh-Hyun embraced his predicament and served as an ambassador for Joseon. He started a business (trading and farming), and through it, he bought back hundreds of enslaved people of Joseon with the money he earned. Moreover, his eyes became opened to the Western world and even to Catholicism, so much so that he had second thoughts about the Confucius ideologies. After eight years in Manchuria, he came home a changed man and with new visions and hopes for his country. However, his dreams did not stand a chance. Three days after his return, he was poisoned by his father, the king, who was unhappy about his western ideas, unhappy about his son's rapport with the Qing Empire, and unhappy about his popularity with the common people. And when he died, it can be said that the dreams of a better and stronger Joseon died with him. For the next two hundred years, Joseon would only get weaker and weaker due to the unpragmatic Confucius ideals and due to constant infighting among the rivaling factions. And the curtains would finally close on Joseon in 1910—that was when Japan took over the nation.

20. WAKING UP IN THE MIDDLE OF THE NIGHT

반밤중 혼자 일어

Lee, (J+au+ng)-(Hw+ahn) | Lee, Jeong-Hwan | 이정환 (1613-1673): Joseon 조선시대

반밤중 혼자 일어
묻노라 이내 꿈아

만리요양을
어느덧 다녀온고

반갑다 학가선용을
친히 뵌듯 하여라

말 뜻 풀이 ★ Word Study in Korean

반밤중에: 한밤중에 | 혼자 이러 물노라: 혼자 일어나 (나의 꿈에게) 물어본다 | 이내 꿈아: 나의 꿈이여 |

만리요양을: 만리나 되는 머나먼 심양을 (만주, 청나라 수도) | 어느덧 다녀온고: 언제 다녀왔느냐 |

반갑다: 반갑구나 | 학가선용을: 소현세자와 봉림왕자를; 학가: 세자나 임금님께서 타시는 수레, 선용: 신선의 얼굴 |

친히 뵌듯 하여라: (꿈에서라도) 직접 만나뵌 것 같구나

반밤중
(bah+n)-(bah+m)-joong
in the middle of the night

혼자 일어
(hoh+n)-jah il-au
waking up

묻노라
mood-noh-rah
I ask

이내 꿈아
ee-neh (GG+oo)-mah
my dear dream

만리요양을
(mah+n)-lee-yoh-(yah+ng)-(eu+l)
that place Shenyang which is more than ten thousand miles away

어느덧
au-(n+eu)-(d+au+d)
when

다녀온고
dah-(n+y+au)-(oh+n)-goh
did you visit and come back

반갑다
(bah+n)-(gah+b)-dah
what a delight it is

학가선용을
(hah+g)-gah-(s+au+n)-(yoh+ng)-(eu+l)
the noble faces (princes) in their royal carriage

친히 뵌듯 하여라
chin-hee (b+wen)-(d+eu+d) hah-(y+au)-rah
it seems as if I have met them in person

NOW TRY TO PUT IT IN YOUR OWN WORDS!

FOR EXAMPLE:

I woke up in the middle of the night and beckoned to my Dream.

"Dream, I can't believe it! Don't tell me you that traveled all the way to Shenyang

and made it back by midnight!"

[It did! It made that long trip in a mere few hours!]

I'm delighted! I feel as if I have gone there myself and have met them (the princes) in person!

CONTEMPLATION:

A heartfelt longing for the princes held as hostages in Shenyang, the capital city of the Qing Empire

MEET THE POET: **Lee, (J+au+ng)-(Hw+ahn)** (an official who stayed pent up at home after Joseon bowed down to the Qing Empire)
Lee (Jau+ng)-(Hw+ahn) refused to leave his home. He retired unofficially, never to set his foot again in the capital city of Hanyang, never to take up his post. Why? Let's just say that the humiliating defeat of the 2nd Manchu Invasion (of Joseon) knocked the wind out of him. He stayed home all day, every day, bemoaning the loss of the two princes taken far away as hostages. He composed poem after poem (ten poems in fact) most of which lamented the fate of the royal sons. He was beyond himself with grief and worry as he had no news about their state or well-being. (Remember, telephones and emails were not invented yet.) Therefore, how glad he must have been when he met them, albeit in a dream!

Did you know that there are more
Sijo, Shijo, Goshijo books to love?
Five stars for becoming culture savvy!
Collect them all today!

 On Patriotic Loyalty
Late Goryeo & Early Joseon Period

On Everything Political
Mid-Joseon Period

On the Matters of
the Heart, Mind, & Soul

On Timeless Reflections
& Everything Wise

Hardcover: 978-1-952082-72-6
Softcover: 978-1-952082-73-3
Ebook: 978-1-952082-74-0

Hardcover: 978-1-952082-78-8
Softcover: 978-1-952082-79-5
Ebook: 978-1-952082-80-1

Hardcover: 978-1-952082-75-7
Softcover: 978-1-952082-76-4
Ebook: 978-1-952082-77-1

Hardcover: 978-1-952082-82-5
Softcover: 978-1-952082-81-8
Ebook: 978-1-952082-83-2

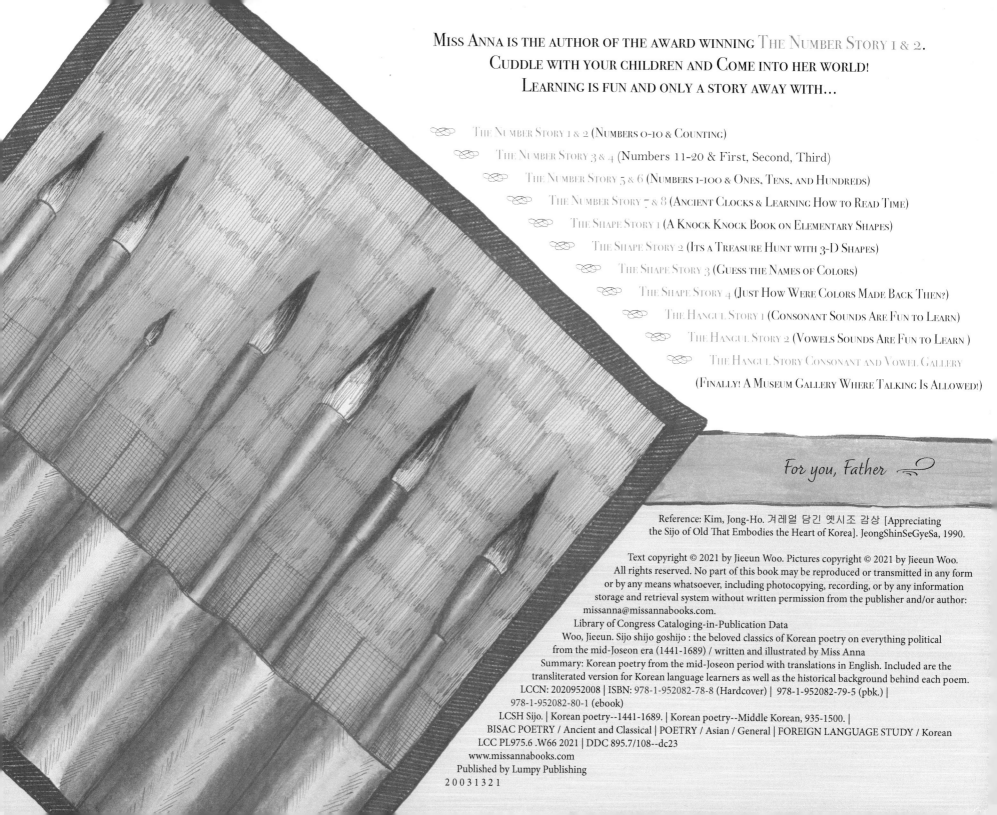

MISS ANNA IS THE AUTHOR OF THE AWARD WINNING THE NUMBER STORY 1 & 2.
CUDDLE WITH YOUR CHILDREN AND COME INTO HER WORLD!
LEARNING IS FUN AND ONLY A STORY AWAY WITH…

THE NUMBER STORY 1 & 2 (NUMBERS 0-10 & COUNTING)

THE NUMBER STORY 3 & 4 (Numbers 11-20 & First, Second, Third)

THE NUMBER STORY 5 & 6 (NUMBERS 1-100 & ONES, TENS, AND HUNDREDS)

THE NUMBER STORY 7 & 8 (ANCIENT CLOCKS & LEARNING HOW TO READ TIME)

THE SHAPE STORY 1 (A KNOCK KNOCK BOOK ON ELEMENTARY SHAPES)

THE SHAPE STORY 2 (ITS A TREASURE HUNT WITH 3-D SHAPES)

THE SHAPE STORY 3 (GUESS THE NAMES OF COLORS)

THE SHAPE STORY 4 (JUST HOW WERE COLORS MADE BACK THEN?)

THE HANGUL STORY 1 (CONSONANT SOUNDS ARE FUN TO LEARN)

THE HANGUL STORY 2 (VOWELS SOUNDS ARE FUN TO LEARN)

THE HANGUL STORY CONSONANT AND VOWEL GALLERY

(FINALLY! A MUSEUM GALLERY WHERE TALKING IS ALLOWED!)

For you, Father

Reference: Kim, Jong-Ho. 겨레얼 담긴 옛시조 감상 [Appreciating the Sijo of Old That Embodies the Heart of Korea]. JeongShinSeGyeSa, 1990.

Library of Congress Cataloging-in-Publication Data
Woo, Jieeun. Sijo shijo goshijo : the beloved classics of Korean poetry on everything political from the mid-Joseon era (1441-1689) / written and illustrated by Miss Anna
Summary: Korean poetry from the mid-Joseon period with translations in English. Included are the transliterated version for Korean language learners as well as the historical background behind each poem.
LCCN: 2020952008 | ISBN: 978-1-952082-78-8 (Hardcover) | 978-1-952082-79-5 (pbk.) | 978-1-952082-80-1 (ebook)
LCSH Sijo. | Korean poetry--1441-1689. | Korean poetry--Middle Korean, 935-1500. |
BISAC POETRY / Ancient and Classical | POETRY / Asian / General | FOREIGN LANGUAGE STUDY / Korean
LCC PL975.6 .W66 2021 | DDC 895.7/108--dc23
www.missannabooks.com
Published by Lumpy Publishing
2 0 0 3 1 3 2 1